MAKING
GREAT KIDS
Greater

To the gifted and talented students and their parents who have shared their lives, their problems, their joys, and their commitments to make a difference with me. And to my graduate students who read the chapters in this book and added suggestions and comments, and most importantly their teacher voices.

MAKING GREAT KIDS
GREAT KIDS
Greater

Easing the Burden of Being Gifted

Dorothy A. Sisk
Foreword by Linda Silverman

CORWIN PRESS
A SAGE Company

For information:

Corwin Press
A SAGE Publications Company
2455 Teller Road
Thousand Oaks, California 91320
www.corwinpress.com

SAGE Publications Ltd.
1 Oliver's Yard
55 City Road
London EC1Y 1SP
United Kingdom

SAGE Publications India Pvt. Ltd.
B 1/I 1 Mohan Cooperative
   Industrial Area
Mathura Road, New Delhi 110 044
India

SAGE Publications Asia-Pacific Pte. Ltd.
33 Pekin Street #02-01
Far East Square
Singapore 048763

Printed in the United States of America.

Library of Congress Cataloging-in-Publication Data

Sisk, Dorothy A.
Making great kids greater : easing the burden of being gifted/Dorothy A. Sisk; foreword by Linda Silverman.
      p. cm.
Includes bibliographical references and index.
ISBN 978-1-4129-5871-4 (cloth)
ISBN 978-1-4129-5872-1 (pbk.)
   1. Gifted children—Social conditions. 2. Gifted children—Psychology.
3. Gifted children—Education. I. Title.

HQ773.5.S543 2009
371.95—dc22   2008017845

This book is printed on acid-free paper.

08   09   10   11   12   10 9 8   7   6   5   4   3   2   1

Acquisitions Editor:	David Chao
Editorial Assistant:	Mary Dang
Production Editor:	Jane Haenel
Copy Editor:	Trey Thoelcke
Typesetter:	C&M Digitals (P) Ltd.
Proofreader:	Ellen Brink
Indexer:	Gloria Tierney
Cover and Graphic Designer:	Rose Storey

Contents

Foreword

Dorothy Sisk is a venerable giant in the field of gifted education, enlightening us over the years regarding the moral sensitivity, creativity, leadership ability, and spiritual development of the gifted. Her newest book, *Making Great Kids Greater: Easing the Burden of Being Gifted*, is a treasure for gifted young people, as well as their parents, teachers, counselors, mentors, and friends. This book integrates insights regarding the social and emotional characteristics of the gifted, brain research, Dabrowski's Theory of Positive Disintegration, and the rich literature on planetary consciousness. Dorothy has the gift of making complex concepts accessible to the reader.

Teachers will find this volume a gold mine of effective classroom strategies to develop the affective domain. Gifted adults will discover themselves in these pages. Anyone interested in the emotional development of the gifted will be delighted by the contents of *Making Great Kids Greater*. Asynchrony, perfectionism, moral courage, sensitivity, empathy, creativity, reflective thinking, tranquility, balance, and meaning are all explored. The book is replete with wonderful examples of children from Dorothy's long career, as well as the voices of teachers.

A lifelong learner, Dorothy obtained a second doctoral degree in psychology, studying the overexcitabilities of teenage gifted girls in a summer program that she designed. This research informs the first chapter of this book. In the second chapter, she elaborates on the distinction between socialization and social development, providing excellent strategies for building positive social development. The discussions of mentors, biographical study, journaling, and bibliotherapy make Chapter 2 particularly useful for teachers.

The third chapter deals with the bane of giftedness: perfectionism. Dorothy describes the difference between healthy and dysfunctional perfectionism, and provides curriculum materials, self-regulation projects, and simulation games for the classroom. Counselors and therapists will appreciate her ideas for group discussion of attitudes about perfectionism. Moral courage takes center stage in Chapter 4. Counselors, teachers, and parents will learn more about dealing with moral dilemmas, overcoming fears, and helping children establish core values. Again, the study of eminent individuals comes into play as a means of introducing students to moral exemplars.

"Know Thyself" is the focus of Chapter 5. Sociodrama, role-playing, and activities to build self-understanding are among the strategies offered to help children learn more about their emotions, talents and actions. In Chapter 6, the sensitivity and empathy of the gifted are explored. Problem-based projects and social action activities allow gifted students to overcome feelings of hopelessness and helplessness. Anyone who works with young people will enjoy learning about care pairs, journaling, identifying helpers, modeling, perspective taking, and activism for young people.

In Chapter 7, the reader encounters reflective thinking. This powerful chapter enables children and teachers to understand how to reprogram the brain for self-efficacy. Chapter 8 is packed with teaching methods for enhancing the creativity of students. While teachers are shown how to identify creatively gifted children, they will be able to use these ideas with all students. Chapter 9 describes strategies for attaining peace, tranquility, mindfulness, and higher consciousness. Negotiation and conflict resolution techniques are addressed. All readers will benefit from this chapter. The book ends with a chapter on achieving balance and finding purpose. The moral exemplars described are inspirational.

Gifted individuals can make a difference in the world. This book provides a road map of how to channel empathy and compassion into a life of service.

Linda Silverman
Director of the Gifted Development Center
Denver, Colorado

Acknowledgments

Avery special thanks to:

Dr. Juliana Townsend Gensley, a member of the original Terman study, who was my first professor in gifted education, and a lifelong colleague in the National Association for Gifted Education.

Ms. Jean Delp, Supervisor of Gifted Education in the Garden Grove School District in California, who inspired me and all of her teachers of the gifted to understand the uniqueness of gifted children and how fragile and vulnerable they are in their giftedness.

Dr. Ernest Boyer, Commissioner of Education, who identified the gifted as one of seven programs to "spotlight" in the U.S. Department of Education, and accepted nothing less than total commitment and effort on behalf of students from his program directors.

Dr. Doris Shallcross, who provided new lenses to see creativity and provided a phenomenal role model for dedication to the Creative Education Foundation, and to her students and colleagues.

Dr. Alexinia Baldwin, who has worked with me in the National Association for Gifted Children (NAGC) and in the World Council of Gifted and Talented (WCGT) to help ensure that the at-risk and culturally different gifted are identified and assisted in reaching their potential.

To Dr. Harry Passow and Dr. James Gallagher, who as presidents of the WCGT demonstrated scholarship and wisdom in working with our international members. It was a pleasure to work with both of these leaders in gifted education.

Dr. E. Paul Torrance, who challenged me to search for answers and begin a journey of understanding the spiritual nature of gifted students.

Dr. Linda Silverman and my cohorts in the Global Awareness Division of the National Association for Gifted and Talented for sharing their knowledge, as they continue to inspire me.

Alllyson Sharp for her continued support and belief in the book.

David Chao for his assistance on the logistics.

Mary Dang for keeping me on schedule.

To the many members of the American Creativity Association, the Creative Education Foundation, The Association for Gifted and Talented (TAG), the National Association for Gifted and Talented, and the WCGT, who allowed me to serve in a leadership role in their organizations; I am honored to have been among so many scholars who share a commitment to gifted children everywhere.

To the hundreds of teachers at the University of South Florida, and at Lamar University, with whom I have had the opportunity to work, for you have been my inspiration. In workshops and classes, I learn as much from the teachers as hopefully they learn from me, and together we demonstrate that learning can be fun and exciting.

To the gifted students in the summer residential programs of the Florida Governors Program, the Texas Governors Program, and the Texas Honors Leadership Program, you have truly been "my teacher" in learning about the needs of gifted students, and you have reinforced my belief that you are truly the hope for the future.

PUBLISHER'S ACKNOWLEDGMENTS

Corwin Press would also like to acknowledge the following for their contributions:

Lauri Kirsch, Ed.D.
Supervisor, K–12 Gifted
Hillsborough County Public Schools
Tampa, FL

Starr Cline, Ed.D.
Adjunct Assistant Professor of Counseling, Research,
Special Education, and Rehabilitation
Hofstra University
Hempstead, NY

About the Author

Dorothy A. Sisk, PhD, holds an endowed chair in education of gifted students at Lamar University in Beaumont, Texas. Throughout her career, she has been intensely involved with the education of gifted and talented children. Dr. Sisk is an international consultant focusing on leadership, communication, and creativity development. She was a professor at the University of South Florida, coordinating programs for training teachers of the gifted, and former director of the U.S. Office of Gifted and Talented in Washington, DC. She currently directs the C. W. Conn and Dorothy Ann Conn Gifted Child Center at Lamar University, and teaches the courses for endorsement in gifted education. She received the Distinguished Leader Award from the Creative Education Foundation (CEF) in 1989, the Distinguished Service Award from the National Association for Gifted Children (NAGC) in 1983 and 1994, the Creative Lifetime Award from CEF in 1994, and was selected for the Hall of Fame Award of CEF in 2005.

Dr. Sisk served as one of the founders and the first president of the American Creativity Association, and president of The Association for Gifted and Talented (TAG), the Florida Association for Gifted, and the World Council for Gifted and Talented, where she also was executive administrator, and editor of *Gifted International* from 1980–1990. She specialized in the field of gifted education, creative behavior, leadership development, and multicultural training. She has conducted training sessions throughout the United States and internationally. Dr. Sisk is author of *Creative Teaching of the Gifted*; coauthor with Doris Shallcross of *Leadership: Making Things Happen, The Growing Person,* and *Intuition: An Inner Way of Knowing*; coauthor with E. Paul Torrance of *Gifted Children in the Regular Classroom* and *Spiritual Intelligence: Developing Higher Level Consciousness;* and coauthor with Susan Israel and Cathy Block of *Collaborative Literacy: Using Gifted Strategies to Enrich Learning for Every Student.* In addition, she has contributed numerous articles and chapters in books on gifted education, creativity, and leadership development.

Introduction

Asynchrony means being "out of sync." Gifted kids are more advanced than kids of their chronological age, which represents one type of asynchrony they experience. In addition, there can be discrepancies between their mental age and their emotional and social development. Silverman (2002) stressed that for a gifted kid to have the mental maturity of a 14-year-old and the physical maturity of an 8-year-old poses enormous emotional and social challenges. Lewis Terman (1931), a pioneer in gifted education recognized this problem of asynchrony and said:

> Precocity unavoidably complicates the problem of social adjustment. The child of eight years with a mentality of twelve or fourteen is faced with a situation almost inconceivably difficult. In order to adjust normally, such a child has to have an exceptionally well-balanced personality and to be well nigh a social genius. The higher the IQ, the more acute the problem. (p. 579)

Along with their asynchrony, the gifted have a unique perception of themselves and their world in comparison to their age mates. The gifted are sensitive, perfectionistic, and intense, and moral issues affect gifted students more deeply and at an earlier age than their peers. Gifted students may appear to be great kids and well adjusted, receiving good grades in school, but they still may suffer from feelings of inadequacy because their successes fall short of their ideals. This book addresses the unique perception of gifted students and suggests ways that great kids can become greater, thus easing the burden of being gifted.

The field of gifted education has focused on the theoretical framework of J. P. Guilford to understand the dimensions of gifted, and on the theories of Carl Rogers and Abraham Maslow to understand the need for gifted students to develop self-understanding and work toward self-actualization. This book emphasizes the use of Kazimierz Dabrowski's Theory of Emotional Development, also known as the Theory of Positive Disintegration, in an attempt to clarify the intensities of gifted students, and to build an understanding of the five "overexcitabilities" as positive energy that can enable the gifted to live lives deeply imbued with immutable values, and to have the moral courage to become their best selves (Silverman, 1993). In short, the five overexcitabilities are: (1) psychomotor, (2) sensual, (3) intellectual, (4) imaginational, and (5) emotional. Dabrowski's theory is being increasingly recognized in the field of gifted education as a means of building greater understanding of gifted individuals.

This book will be helpful for teachers, parents, and counselors, but most important for gifted students, as they read and recognize themselves on the pages. Chapters include case studies and practical suggestions, including a "Teacher Voice" representing a teacher's reflection on the material in the chapter. This is followed by a section called "Read On," "Log On," and "Reflect On" to extend the use and understanding of the material. Research is integrated into each chapter to build a foundation for the suggested activities and strategies that parents, teachers, and counselors can use with gifted students.

The introductory chapter discusses the unique perception of the gifted in the context of Dabrowski's five overexcitabilities, and introduces his concept of multilevelness. The second chapter deals with the need for gifted students to develop social skills and makes a distinction between socialization and social development, and how these terms are often used interchangeably. Socialization is a Level II function in Dabrowski's Theory of Emotional Development in which the individual goes along with the group, whereas social development represents a multilevel function in Levels IV–V in which the individual is seeking autonomy, responsibility, and authenticity.

The third chapter discusses perfectionism in gifted students, which Dabrowski viewed as a positive trait. A distinction is made between debilitating perfectionism and the positive side of perfectionism in seeking excellence. The fourth chapter addresses the need for gifted students to develop moral courage and suggests ways gifted students can learn to live deeply with immutable values.

The fifth chapter focuses on individuality and how gifted students can take charge of their lives to become aware of their gifts, and it suggests ways for gifted students to develop their unique individual qualities. The sixth chapter discusses the sensitivity and empathy gifted students have for others, as well as how they can build their capacity to be other-centered rather than self-centered. This chapter stresses the need for gifted students to alleviate their sense of helplessness that comes from their empathy for the suffering of others. Activities to develop and maintain their sensitivity and empathy for others are provided, including activism for gifted students.

The seventh chapter focuses on reflective thinking and its relationship to building a strong sense of self-efficacy in gifted students. The skills involved in changing one's thinking are addressed, with the use of the computer as a metaphor for the brain and examples of gifted students who have used these skills are provided. The eighth chapter discusses the importance of gifted students developing their creativity and how they can further develop their creative ability in problem solving.

The ninth chapter discusses the importance of developing a sense of peace and tranquility, and it suggests ways gifted students can develop their ability to go within for "inner dialogue." This chapter also explores the need for gifted students to walk away from controversy and to become an example for peace-making and conflict resolution. The tenth and final chapter discusses the importance of gifted students achieving balance in their lives to develop a sense of moderation to avoid the extremes in physical, mental, or emotional aspects of life, and the importance of identifying purpose and ways to live a meaningful life.

The intensities need to be viewed and presented positively to gifted children and youth as strengths to enable them to understand and value their gifts. Gifted students need the help and support of significant adults in their lives, their teachers and parents, and this book will help to build an understanding of the uniqueness of gifted students. The content of the chapters was selected to provide a window into the inner world of giftedness, including their unique perception, their need for social development rather than socialization, their sensitivity and empathy for others, their need for reflective thinking, their creativity, their need to experience peace and tranquility, and their need to achieve balance in their lives and to identify their purpose.

As a teacher and counselor of gifted students, a director of teacher training in gifted education, a national director of the Office of Gifted and Talented, and most important as a parent of a gifted son, I observed their uniqueness and their attempts to mask their giftedness to try and fit in. It is my intention that this book ease the burden of being gifted and enable gifted students to use their gifts to bring not only themselves, but society to a higher set of values and action.

REFERENCES

Silverman, L. (1993). Techniques for preventive counseling. In L. K. Silverman (Ed.), *Counseling the gifted and talented* (pp. 81–111). Denver, CO: Love.

Silverman, L. (2002). Asynchronous development. In M. Neihart, S. Reis, M. Robinson, & S. Moon (Eds.), *The social and emotional development of gifted children: What do we know?* (pp. 31–37). Waco, TX: Prufrock Press.

Terman, L. (1931). The gifted child. In C. Murchinson (Ed.), *A handbook of child psychology* (pp. 568–584). Worcester, MA: Clark University Press.

1

Gifted Kids Have a Unique Perception

Gifted kids have a unique way of perceiving their world and their relationship to it, and this unique perception is probably the first indicator that teachers and parents have of their giftedness. As young children, they can make abstract connections and synthesize a variety of experiences to make both sophisticated and practical conclusions far beyond what is expected of their age (Silverman, 1993). In an enrichment program at a local university, a graduate class of puppeteers were planning to demonstrate a performance of Hansel and Gretel using life-size puppets. The organizing professor and director of the group stressed that only upper grade children should attend; but, I urged him to allow all of the children to be included, even the kindergarten students. He agreed, only if they used appropriate theater etiquette. I asked each teacher to prepare his or her children for "theater manners" before they attended the performance. The kindergarten teacher, an insightful and creative individual, brought her children forward to their conversation rug, and said: "I am so exited about our visit to the theater. I plan to run in and jump on chairs, bounce around, and shout out my enthusiasm for being included—yippee."

From the back of the circle of children, Mandy quietly said with a serious tone, "And you'll never be asked back again." To this response, the teacher replied, "What should I do?" and the children began sharing ideas, including the importance of walking in quietly, sitting in their seats, and listening. Mandy added, "Sort of like church manners, but this will be more fun."

Mandy's teacher described her as always seeming to see things differently from the other children, and as a result they tended to isolate her.

Mandy had an advanced level of moral reasoning, and it was very important to her that things be fair. She could be judgmental, and expected the teacher to settle disputes. She would loudly call out to her teacher, "You are needed over here," which often represented a response to Mandy's perception of the other children being insensitive, cruel, or even unfair in their interactions with one another. Linda Silverman, a psychologist and director of the Gifted Development Center in Denver, Colorado, observed that, in the field of gifted education, it is often not well known that giftedness has an emotional as well as a cognitive substructure, and that gifted children not only think differently from other children, but they also feel differently. This difference in feeling can be explained as an intensity or expanded field of subjective experience (Silverman, 1993).

In this chapter, we examine the unique perception of gifted students in the context of the Dabrowski Theory of Emotional Development. The theory's five overexcitabilities—psychomotor, sensual, intellectual, imaginational, and emotional—are discussed, with examples of student responses on the Overexcitability Questionnaire. The second component of Dabrowski's theory of multilevelness is then introduced, with the five levels, ranging from Level I to Level V.

THE DABROWSKI THEORY OF EMOTIONAL DEVELOPMENT

According to Kazimierz Dabrowski, a Polish psychiatrist and psychologist, who developed his Theory of Emotional Development (also known as the Theory of Positive Disintegration), emotional intensity is a positive characteristic for gifted children and gifted adults (Dabrowski, 1964). He described emotional development as an interaction between developmental potential and the environment. He called this intensity *overexcitability* and identified five types.

1. *Psychomotor*—restlessness, curiosity, and lots of energy
2. *Sensual*—pleasure in sensory and aesthetic experiences
3. *Intellectual*—higher level thinking (analysis and synthesis); asks lots of questions
4. *Imaginational*—spontaneous; fantasizes and uses imagery and metaphor
5. *Emotional*—intense feelings; is sensitive and empathetic

Dabrowski (1902–1980) survived both world wars, and during the second, he risked his life to provide asylum to Jews escaping from the Nazis. The Nazis and the communists imprisoned, tortured, and prevented him from continuing his professional work as a psychiatrist and psychologist. Dabrowski's Theory of Emotional Development grew out of his own experiences with injustice, death, and suffering, while at the same time he witnessed incredible acts of self-sacrifice in the midst of inhumanity and cruelty. Dabrowski was appalled at what he observed in the world around him, and he began to study the biographies of eminent people to identify the universal values that he was seeking in his own life.

Piechowski (2006) said that Dabrowski was inspired by Socrates, Gandhi, and Kierkegaard, and by the great saints who went through agonies similar to his own. In his research, Dabrowski noted the relationship between cognition and emotion, and the heightened intensity of gifted and creative individuals. He said these intensities, or overexcitabilities (OEs), could be thought of as a great deal of physical, sensual, creative, intellectual, and emotional energy that may result in creative work, as well as advanced emotional and ethical development in adults. When OEs are considered in this way, they can be a positive force for gifted children and adults, as they enrich, empower, and amplify individual gifts and talents (Dabrowski & Piechowski, 1977; Piechowski, 1979; Piechowski, 2006). Without some degree of intensity in the five OEs, talent is mere technical facility lacking heart and fire (Piechowski, 2002). Dabrowski's theory and his concept of overexcitabilities represent a framework for self-efficacy and a child's potential (Meckstroth, 1999).

What Does Research Say About Dabrowski's Theory?

Research comparing OEs has found greater incidence of them in gifted children and adults than in comparison populations (Felder, 1982; Piechowski & Colangelo, 1984; Piechowski, Silverman, & Falk, 1985; Schiever, 1985; Gallagher, 1986). Shirley Schiever (1985) used the Overexcitability Questionnaire (OEQ) to explore the relationship between OEQ profiles and creativity in gifted middle school students. She worked with 21 seventh grade students who were enrolled in a gifted program. The students were administered the OEQ and the Something About Myself (SAM), which is part of the Khatena-Torrance Creative Perception Inventory (Khatena & Torrance, 1976). Shiever grouped the students into high creative and low creative groups using their scores on the SAM, and compared their SAM scores to the OEQ. She found that high creative students scored significantly higher on imaginational, emotional, and intellectual OEs.

Cheryl Ackerman (1997) conducted an exploratory study to assess the use of the Overexcitability Questionnaire as an alternative method of identifying gifted students. She worked with 79 high school students, in which 42 were identified as gifted. She found that the group of students that had been identified as gifted had an OEQ profile that contained higher scores on psychomotor, intellectual, and emotional OEs. Ackerman also found that the psychomotor OE contributed to the differentiation between the gifted and nongifted students.

Joan Smutny, founder and director of the Center for Gifted at National-Louis University in Evanston, Illinois, described how emotional intensity causes gifted children to sense the joys, pains, sorrows, and hopes of family members, friends, and classmates. She observed that gifted children sometimes become distressed when they cannot alleviate the problems of others (Smutny, 1998). This observation helps to explain Mandy's urgency in calling her teacher to make things right.

OVEREXCITABILITIES

Gifted children have an expanded awareness that derives primarily from the emotional, intellectual, and imaginational OEs, and can eventually lead to the development of value structures that guide their development in adolescence and adulthood. This developing value system and the OEs create a unique inner life and perception that marks the gifted as different from their peer group (Silverman, 1993).

Dabrowski found that his professional colleagues wanted to "fix" individuals with OEs; yet, he argued that OEs can be viewed as powerful inner forces to be used for the development of creativity and giftedness. Even today, a child with psychomotor overexcitability may be misdiagnosed as hyperactive, or as having attention deficit disorder; yet, these same children are capable of intense concentration in areas of their interest (Webb, 2000). Their surplus of energy can be noted in rapid speech and gestures, as well as in their enjoyment of fast games and sports. However, this high energy may be problematic in the classroom, and many teachers report that working with gifted children with high energy can be mentally exhausting after a full day of interaction with them. Elizabeth Maxwell, associate director of the Gifted Child Development Center in Denver, Colorado, said that overexcitabilities and intensities can startle and alarm others, and these behaviors are not easy to live with, but they do make life interesting (Maxwell, 1995).

Imaginational Overexcitability

Imaginational OE can be observed in the frequent use of images and metaphors. Young gifted children may mix truth and fiction, and they talk about elaborate dreams and illusions as if they have actually occurred. In my first year of teaching, a fellow teacher described a child—let's call her Lydia—as a "liar." She said, "Lydia, is constantly talking about wild happenings and just flat out tells lies." When I first met this youngster, a third grade student, I asked all of the children to introduce themselves with their name, and to share something that was fun or enjoyable for them. I explained this would help me get to know them better. When Lydia spoke, she said, "My name is Lydia, and my mother baked a cake for my birthday, and a clown jumped out of the cake for me, and sang 'Happy Birthday.'" All of the students groaned, and one said, "That is so stupid; it could never happen." Luckily, none of the students labeled her statements as a "lie." I quickly replied, "What a wonderful imagination you have; when we have story time or need fresh ideas in creative writing, I will call on you for help." And I did. Soon the negative feelings the class held for Lydia were dispelled, and with affirmation of her imaginational OE, she became the class resource for imagination.

Intellectual Overexcitability

Intellectual OE can be observed in children and adults who ask lots of questions, and think about their thinking. People with intellectual OE are very introspective; they ponder and analyze, and they are capable of sustained attention. They usually love to read, and are keen on detailed planning. In that same first-year classroom was another gifted student who was fascinated and knowledgeable about dinosaurs. One day, when he was holding forth about the triceratops, I know my mouth was hanging open, and he paused, saying, "You know why I like your class, Miss Denning? You still want to learn." Intellectual OEs are always eager and ready to oblige. As a result of their avid reading and interest, they usually have a rich fund of information to share with others and to use in pursuit of their own interests.

Sensual Overexcitability

Sensual OEs have heightened sensory experiences and pleasure in seeing, smelling, tasting, touching, and hearing. They appreciate beautiful objects and are fascinated by words and writing styles. These individuals, as young children, are the ones who simultaneously suck their thumbs and caress the satin on their blanket or Daddy's old tie. Sensual OEs enjoy certain smells, and often they have distinct notions about them. They are sensitive to labels on shirts, or certain fabrics that they describe as "itchy," and they may reject certain foods because of their texture.

Emotional Overexcitability

Emotional OEs have intense feelings and extreme emotions. They have strong emotional ties and attachments to others, and to their environment. This attachment to an environment may make it difficult for these OEs to adjust to new places. Their sensitivity to relationships and empathy for others can be manifested in tears; for example, when another student is reprimanded or disciplined in the classroom, this can be devastating for an emotional OE. They have intense affective memories, particularly of memories and feelings associated with their personal life events.

Psychomotor Overexcitability

Psychomotor OEs are restless and have lots of energy. They have rapid speech and sometimes will put several words together as one word. Psychomotor OEs are often compulsive talkers and chatter away in the classroom. In group activities, they press for action and urge others to get started. Psychomotor OEs love games and fast sports, like soccer and baseball, and they can be impulsive with their marked enthusiasm. Foot twirling, fidgeting, and drumming on the desk are other manifestations of psychomotor OE, and these students can be mistaken as hyperactive or classified as having attention deficit disorder (Webb, 2000).

HOW OTHERS PERCEIVE THE GIFTED: IS IT A CHEETAH?

The unique perception of the gifted has been examined, and the way they perceive the world differently is manifested in their intensity. Stephanie Tolan, author and mother of a gifted child, explored how others perceive the gifted and she observed that it is a tough time to raise, teach, or be a highly gifted child. Tolan used the cheetah as a metaphor for the gifted. She said, just as we think of a cheetah first because of its speed, upward to 70 mph, we think of giftedness in terms of achievement in academics. I would add we also think of it in terms of acceptable behavior, which often does not include the overexcitabilities. Tolan noted that cheetahs are not always running, and can't maintain their top speed for long periods without considerable rest; yet, they are still cheetahs. She stressed that gifted children who may not be achieving are still gifted, even though they may not be identified for gifted programs (Tolan, 2003).

PERSONAL EXPERIENCES OF OEs

Leslie Sword, an Australian consultant in gifted education shared an example of how emotional OEs can be misunderstood at the 2002 World Council for Gifted and Talented (WCGT) meeting in Adelaide, Australia (Sword, 2002). She said Rebecca (aged 8) displayed her emotional OE while working on a drawing in class by suddenly throwing it to the ground, stamping on it, and bursting into tears, shouting, "It's not right, I can't do it right." Her teacher was appalled by this outburst and recommended Rebecca not be promoted to the next year because she was emotionally immature.

Another example of intellectual OE provided by Sword was Annabel (aged 6) who taught herself to read and write before starting school. She loved reading, particularly reading *The Hobbit*. In her first year of school, she was made to read at the first grade level of the other children, and she became withdrawn. Her teacher described her as having poor social skills. In her second year, Annabel became angry and frustrated with school, and began misbehaving and disrupting the class. The second grade teacher recommended that Annabel receive counseling for her oppositional and antisocial behavior.

To illustrate imaginational OE, the classic story of a student—let's call him Paul—will be helpful in understanding the importance of nurturing this OE. Paul loved to draw and his pictures were full of color, motion, and other indications of a lively imagination. When he entered kindergarten, his teacher asked the children to draw a flower, and she displayed a large red flower with a green stem as a model. Paul enthusiastically began drawing purple flowers, blue flowers, and yellow flowers in a field of green grass. The teacher frowned and held up his picture as an example of not following directions. She asked Paul to draw a large red flower with a green stem. Unhappily he did so. The next year, Paul's family moved to another city, and the teacher asked the class to use their imagination and to draw wonderful flowers. Paul drew a flower with a large red head and a green stem.

Sensual OEs have heightened experiences with their senses, and they experience life deeply through seeing, smelling, tasting, touching, and hearing. School can be a very scary place for a young sensual OE. Martha refused to use the toilet at school, and resisted going to bathroom time with her kindergarten class. "It smells," she said. She would soil herself at school, or rush madly to the bathroom when she arrived home. Soon Martha began to cut down on the water she drank, and became severely dehydrated. The school cafeteria was so noisy, she described it as a "wild place" full of noise, and she began to refuse to eat in the cafeteria. When her mother took her to the doctor, he was concerned she could become anorexic, and suggested that Martha's mother work with the school for private bathroom time, and eating lunch in the classroom with the teacher. The school was not willing to make individual concessions for Martha, and the principal recommended referral to the behavioral disorder program. Martha's parents decided to homeschool her until she could overcome or manage her sensual OE. At age 8 she has learned how to screen out excess noise, but she still finds public bathrooms problematic. The school Martha attends today has an odorizer that is activated when someone enters. She says it smells like a doctor's office, but that is better than the other "bathroom smell."

Stanley (aged 12) manifests psychomotor OE, and when he makes a presentation in his middle school class, his entire body is involved. He gestures and speaks very rapidly. Stanley explains his topic in such detail that after the first few minutes, the other students lose interest, and many poke fun of his excessive rapid delivery. They imitate the sound of a machine gun: "ratta-tatta-tat." His teacher describes him as "antsy" and says he always thinks of some excuse to get up and move around in the room. Stanley twists in his chair, drums his fingers on his desk, and swings his foot aimlessly. Needless to say, he receives many teacher discipline referrals for his psychomotor OE, and physical education time is taken away as a punishment, which is a necessary outlet for Stanley's impulsive high energy.

His seventh grade teacher is working with him and the rest of the class on relaxation techniques, and she provides soothing background music in the classroom to establish a "calming" atmosphere for all of the students. Stanley's mother purchased earphones for him to use at home with lots of Mozart music to help calm him for studying and preparation for bedtime. In addition, he has learned to count slowly to ten, and to take deep breaths to help calm himself. In class, Stanley makes PowerPoint presentations with bullet points of information that decrease his excessive and rapid delivery.

IMPORTANCE OF OVEREXCITABILITIES

OEs guide a child's life, shape his or her focus and values, and help create a unique inner life (Meckstroth, 1999). The strength of the OEs combined with special abilities make up a child's developmental potential for self-actualization (Silverman, 1993). When emotional, imaginational, and intellectual OEs surpass sensual and psychomotor OEs in strength, there is great developmental potential for the individual to reach high levels of personality development (Dabrowski, 1972). An examination of student responses on an Overexcitabilities Questionnaire developed by Falk, Lind, Miller, Piechowski, and Silverman. (2003) will help to illustrate the OEs. The OEQ was administered to gifted adolescents in a residential summer program (Sisk, 2006). The students responded to the questionnaire in an untimed setting, and the following selected responses to several of the questions on the OEQ provide a window to build greater understanding of the five OEs.

In response to the question "What kinds of things get your mind going?" the following imaginational OE was made:

> Sometimes when I am imagining something, I can be composing a short musical piece, and my mind usually is filled with music that I have heard or performed, but it is in the moments of internal quiet that I hear new things. (Female, age 16)

In response to the question "What has been your experience of the most intense pleasure?" the following emotional OE was identified:

> Last summer, I worked with the Summer Special Olympics for children with disabilities. We worked hard for weeks and weeks and finally the "big day" came; I was able to see our hard work pay off. To see the pride in these special children's eyes flooded my soul with happiness. (Female, age 17)

The question "When do you feel the most energy and what do you do with it?" elicited this psychomotor OE response:

> I feel tons of energy after I do really well in a race. If I win or improve my track time, I get lots of energy. With all of this newfound energy I usually annoy people. It comes out in the form of hyperness and excitement. (Male, age 16)

In response to the question "How precisely can you visualize events, real or imaginary?" this sensual OE was elicited:

> All the time, I am always trying to create scenes from my surroundings. Sometimes I imagine people that I would like to talk to and—don't laugh—talk to them, much as they did in the movie *Tap*. I listen to the sounds around me and hear music in it. (Male, age 16)

In response to the question, "Do you think about your thinking?" the following intellectual OE was identified:

> I would first find a pattern and follow it. What goes on in my head would be how one solves the problem. Second, I would tell myself that I'm not confused. I would think, why do we have to understand this idea? Last, I would find the pattern. (Female, age 16)

Dabrowski worked on his theory for many years, and there are two major concepts in its foundation, the five overexcitabilities and the multilevelness. The second concept of multilevelness introduces the idea that the emotions, motivations, values, strivings, and behaviors can be examined through a prism of levels.

MULTILEVELNESS

Nancy Miller, the associate editor for the *Advanced Development Journal* published by the Institute for Advanced Development in Denver, Colorado, summarized the multilevels of Dabrowski at the 2006 National Association for Gifted Children (NAGC) conference in Charlotte, North Carolina. She said that in Level I there are no active agents for personality change, and the individual focuses on one's own needs and desires and is ego-centered. In Level II, the individual is responsive to peers and there is a desire for approval. One is guided by custom or expectations of others. In Level III, the individual begins to develop independence from social opinion, and there is a growing critical perception and evaluation of values. In Level IV, the individual begins to be objective and self-evaluate. There is a growing awareness of one's uniqueness and the use of self-designed methods of dealing with stress, anxiety, conflict, and depression. In Level V, the individual identifies with the highest levels of development and is autonomous. In Level V, individuals assume responsibility for others, as well as their own development. Miller (2006) described this multilevelness as a developmental process, as depicted in Figure 1.1.

In the developmental process, the individual moves from external control and impulse in Level II to a developing sense of internal control in Level III with engagement in reflective and critical examination of one's values. In Level II, the individual is responsive to social norms and relative values, and in Level III and IV, one moves away from social opinion and becomes more perceptive and self-evaluative. In Level II, one is competitive

Figure 1.1   Developmental Process of the Multilevels of Dabrowski

External Control	⟶	Internal Control
Impulse	⟶	Reflection
Sociability	⟶	Empathy
Social Norm	⟶	Norm of the Ideal
Relative Values	⟶	Universal Values
Competition	⟶	Service to Others
Individual Love	⟶	All-Embracing Love

Source: Adapted from Dabrowski K., Kawczak, A., & Piechowski, M. M. (1970). *Mental growth through positive disintegration.* London: Gryf.

and strives to "best" others, whereas in Level IV there is movement toward service to others, and movement from individual love in Level II to Level IV and V in which one responds with an all-embracing love. The Dabrowski multilevels are depicted in Table 1.1.

Dabrowski viewed these five different levels as reflections of the potential for individual advanced development, and he used the term *developmental potential*. He said individual development comes through a process of lower cognitive emotional structures being disintegrated into higher level structures.

Piechowski (2002) shared an example of developmental growth in a boy at age 15 and then again at age 17 responding to the question, "Who am I?" The first response was: "I feel that I am a person who is on the earth, that is destined to use his abilities and talents to his fullest" (p. 31).

Piechowski said this response represented an egocentric view of self-actualization at Level II. At age 17, the boy responded to the same question by stating:

> The answer to this question has changed over the past few years. A few years ago, I was a person who wanted things for himself. Now I am trying to change that person to a person who wants to contribute to others and the world, not just himself. Obtaining this type of person in this world is not easy. The one thing that is a roadblock is competition. (p. 31)

This latter response demonstrated the inner conflict that one goes through in an adjustment to higher values, as well as the conflict between

Table 1.1   Dabrowski Multilevels of Development

Level I	Level I individuals lack empathy and self-examination; they tend to blame others when something goes wrong; and they are egocentric and stereotypical.
Level II	Level II individuals display the beginning of shame and extreme or changeable identification with others, with no clear-cut set of self-determined values.
Level III	Level III individuals can become depressed and anxious when they perceive a lack of achievement of their established goals.
Level IV	Level IV individuals manifest high levels of responsibility, reflective judgment, empathy, and authenticity.
Level V	Level V individuals live a life in service to humanity, committed to universal principles; they identify with humanity, and their lives reflect compassion and forgiveness.

Source: Dabrowski, K., & Piechowski, M. (1977). *Theories of levels of emotional development.* Oceanside, NY: Dabor Science.

"besting" others to get ahead and contributing to others. As gifted students reflect on their own behavior and the behavior of others, they will begin to reject the values of the group (Level II) and move toward identifying their own individual values (Level III), and then move toward Level IV in which there is an awareness of one's uniqueness, and what Miller (2006) called existential responsibility.

Goal of the Developmental Process of the Multilevels

Self-knowledge as described by Dabrowski takes time, develops slowly, and involves inner growth for advanced personality development. Gifted students observe others and the way things work in the world, and they reflect, evaluate, and question. They question their own differences in perception and feeling. Advanced personality development results in strong, unique, autonomous, and authentic values and personality structure (Mendaglio & Tillier, 2006). Developmental potential was described by Piechowski (2002) as the capacity for inner transformation as the individual consciously engages in the work of personal growth to become a better person, to become all that one can be, or to self-actualize.

Dabrowski's Theory of Emotional Development is gaining recognition and appreciation among educators who want to better understand and nurture gifted children. Evidence of this was noted in the preconference at the National Association for Gifted Children sponsored by the Global Awareness division in 2006, focusing on the Dabrowski theory and its impact on gifted education.

In the second chapter, we will examine the need for gifted students to develop social skills, making a distinction between socialization and social development. In Dabrowskian terms, socialization is a Level II interaction, and social development is a Level IV–V or multilevel function.

SUMMARY

In this chapter, we examined the unique perception of gifted students in the context of the Dabrowski Theory of Emotional Development, also known as the Theory of Positive Disintegration. A brief biography of Kazimierz Dabrowski was presented, including his imprisonment by the Nazis and the communists for providing asylum to Jews in World War II. Dabrowski's concept of developmental potential includes talents, specific abilities, and intelligence, plus the five overexcitabilities: psychomotor, sensual, intellectual, imaginational, and emotional. The Overexcitability Questionnaire was briefly discussed, and examples of student responses to selected questions on the OEQ were used to demonstrate the five OEs. The five OEs provide talent with its power of invention and expression. The multilevelness in the Dabrowski theory was discussed, and the goal of the developmental process of the multilevels as self-knowledge and

Excellent–Editors' Choice — CNET*

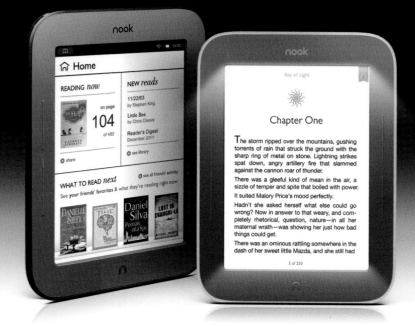

NOOK Simple Touch™
So Easy, Just Touch and Read

NOOK Simple Touch™
with GlowLight™

Perfect for Bed and Bright Sun

NOOK.com

NK103 Rev. 10/2012

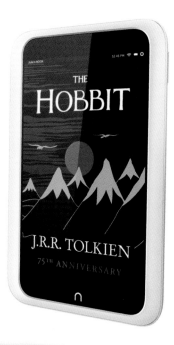

NOOK® HD+
World's Lightest and
Lowest-Priced Full HD 9" Tablet*

NOOK® HD
World's Best
7" Media Tablet

NOOK.com

self-actualization was emphasized. The five levels of Dabrowski were discussed, ranging from Level I, which is totally ego-centered, to Level V, which involves authenticity, autonomy, and responsibility.

Teacher Voice

In all my years of teaching, I was one of the many who would label children with OE behaviors as a behavioral problem. I conformed to what our educational society deems as acceptable/not acceptable behavior without looking at the child as a whole. How could I not see that their outbursts in class were cries for "Stimulate Me!"? Reading through this chapter, I could place one of my students in each example and description of the five overexcitabilities. I will use this information in my classrooms by taking the time to reexamine my criteria for students I label as a problem.

Lisa Morrison
Science teacher, fifth grade

Read On

Kurcinka, M. (1991). *Raising your spirited child: A guide for parents whose child is more intense, sensitive, perceptive, persistent, energetic.* New York: HarperCollins.

Lind, S. (2000). Overexcitability and the highly gifted. *Communicator*, California Association for the Gifted, 3(4), 19, 45–48.

Piechowski, M. (2002). Experiencing in a higher key: Dabrowski's theory of and for the gifted. *Communicator*, California Association for the Gifted, Spring, 28–31, 35–36.

Log On

Dabrowski's Theory of Positive Disintegration. (http://members.shaw.ca/positivedisintegration/). A brief overview of the theory and its relevance to the gifted.

Guidelines for Handling the Dark Side of Emotional Sensitivity in Gifted Children (http://gifted.ucalgary.ca/gifteduc/files/gifteduc/GuidelinesHandlingSM.pdf).

Is It a Cheetah? (http://stephanietolan.com/is_it_a_cheetah.htm). A discussion of giftedness and asynchronous development.

Reflect On

- Think of times when you try to stand back and look at yourself objectively. What do you reflect upon?
- Piechowski (2002) said that it is unfortunate that the stronger the overexcitabilities are, the less peers and teachers welcome them, unless they too are gifted. What are the implications of this statement?
- What has been your experience of the most intense pleasure?
- Because the gifted student's manner of perceiving and experiencing is often viewed as overreacting, it is treated as something that must be cured. What do you think about this statement?

REFERENCES

Ackerman, C. (1997). Identifying gifted adolescents using personality characteristics: Dabrowski's overexcitabilities. *Roeper Review*, *19*, 229–236.

Dabrowski, K. (1964). *Positive disintegration*. Boston: Little, Brown.

Dabrowski, K. (1972). *Psychoneurosis is not an illness*. London: Gryf.

Dabrowski, K., Kawczak, A., & Piechowski, M. M. (1970). *Mental growth through positive disintegration*. London: Gryf

Dabrowski, K. & Piechowski, M. (1977). *Theory of levels of emotional development* (Vols. 1 & 2). Oceanside, NY: Dabor Science.

Falk, R., Lind, S., Miller, B., Piechowski, M., & Silverman, L. (2003). *The overexcitability questionnaire-two (OEQII): Manual, scoring system and questionnaire*. Denver, CO: Institute for the Study of Advanced Development.

Felder, R. (1982). *Responses of gifted education and chemical engineering graduate students on the OEQ & DRI*. Paper presented at the National Association for Gifted Children Conference, New Orleans.

Gallagher, S. A. (1986). A comparison of the concept of over-excitabilities with measures of creativity and school achievement in sixth grade students. *Roeper Review*, *8*, 115–119.

Khatena, J., & Torrance, E. (1976). *Manual for Khatena-Torrance creative personality inventory*. Chicago: Stoelting.

Kurcinka, M. (1991). *Raising your spirited child: A guide for parents whose child is more intense, sensitive, perceptive, persistent, energetic*. New York: HarperCollins.

Lind, S. (2000). Overexcitability and the highly gifted. *Communicator*, California Association for the Gifted, *3*(4), 19, 45–48.

Maxwell, E. (1995). The changing developmental needs of gifted: Birth to maturity. In J. Genshafh, M. Bireley, & C. Hollinger (Eds.), *Serving gifted and talented students: A resource for school personnel*. Austin, TX: Pro-ed.

Meckstroth, E. (1999). Complexities of giftedness: Dabrowski's theory. In J. Smutny (Ed.), *The young gifted child: Potential and promise, an anthology* (pp. 295–307). Creskill, NJ: Hampton Press.

Mendaglio, S., & Tillier, W. (2006). Dabrowski's theory of positive disintegration and giftedness: Overexcitability research findings. *Journal for the Education of the Gifted*. *30*(1), 68–87.

Miller, N. (2006, November 1). *Developmental dynamisms*. Paper presented at the National Association for Gifted, Charlotte, NC.

Piechowski, M. (1979). Developmental potential. In N. Colangelo & R. T. Zaffram (Eds.), *New voices of counseling the gifted* (pp. 25–57). Dubuque, IA: Kendall Hunt.

Piechowski, M. (2002). Experiencing in a higher key: Dabrowski's theory of and for the gifted. *Communicator*, California Association for the Gifted, *33*(1), 31–36.

Piechowski, M. (2006). *Mellow out, they say. If I only could: Intensities and sensitivities of the young and bright*. Madison, WI: Yunasa Books.

Piechowski, M., & Colangelo, N. (1984). Developmental potential of the gifted. *Gifted Child Quarterly*, *28*, 80–88.

Piechowski, M., Silverman, L., & Falk, R. (1985). Comparison of intellectually and artistically gifted on five dimensions of mental functioning. *Perceptions and Motor Skills*. *60*, 539–549.

Shiever, S. (1985). Creative personality characteristics and dimensions of mental functioning in gifted adolescents. *Roeper Review*, *7*, 223–236.

Silverman, L. (1993). The gifted individual. In L. K.Silverman (Ed.), *Counseling the gifted and talented* (pp. 3–28). Denver, CO: Love.

Sisk, D. (2006, November 2). *OEQ results in gifted students*. Paper presented at the National Association for Gifted, Charlotte, NC.

Smutny, J. (1998). Recognizing and honoring the sensitivities of gifted children *Communicator*, California Association for the Gifted, *29*(3), 10–11.

Sword, L. (2002). *Dabrowski applied to counseling*. Paper presented at the World Council for Gifted and Talented meeting in Adelaide, Australia.

Tolan, S. (2003). *Is it a cheetah?* Retrieved March 26, 2008, from http://stephanietolan.com/is_it_a_cheetah.htm

Webb, J. (2000, August 7). *Mis-diagnosis and dual diagnosis of gifted children*. Paper presented at the APA convention, Washington, DC.

2

One Size Does Not Fit All

Socialization vs. Social Development

I limit myself to three answers per class, that way there aren't as many groans when I share my ideas, but when the teacher needs an answer, I sometimes will add another point. When class is over, no one talks to me, and I usually eat alone, or with Timmy, who no one likes either, because he is fat and has really bad body odor.

Michael (age 10)

Michael is a fifth grade gifted student who takes most of his classes in mixed ability student classes, except for an accelerated math class. He has been counseled by both his teachers and his parents to "take a back seat" and "don't answer too many questions" and "stop using big words that other students don't know." His response to these suggestions is, "That would make me, not me. I like to share what I know—I need to share what I know, and to be me, not pretend I don't know."

Michael is a fine example of what the French psychologist Jean Terrassier (1985) called dyssynchrony. He said that dyssynchrony is made up of two parts. One part is internal and refers to disparate rates of development in intellectual, psychomotor, and affective development. The second part of dyssynchrony is social, in which the gifted child feels out-of-step with the social context. In Michael's case, he has advanced information and knowledge that he is being asked to keep to himself, because the other students don't understand or they aren't interested in his ideas.

Lewis Terman (1931), a pioneer in gifted education, identified more than 1,500 age-11 gifted students, and he and his colleagues followed them throughout their lifetime. Terman addressed the issue of dyssynchrony:

> Precocity unavoidably complicates the problem of social adjustment. The child of eight years with a mentality of twelve or fourteen is faced with a situation almost inconceivably difficult. In order to adjust normally, such a child has to have an exceptionally well-balanced personality and to be well nigh a social genius. The higher the IQ, the more acute the problem. (p. 579)

Another early researcher in gifted education, Leta S. Hollingworth (1930) said the further removed gifted children are from the average in intelligence, the more pressing their adjustment problems become. In a study of social adjustment, Hollingworth found gifted adolescents to be much less neurotic, much more self-sufficient, and much less submissive than nongifted adolescents. Yet, she found that as the intelligence of gifted children increased, so did their difficulty with peer relations.

The truism that one size fits all is not appropriate for clothes, educational environments, familial and peer environments, or the sociocultural context. On the surface, it might appear that Michael is not socially adjusted, but he would demonstrate good social adjustment when and if he could find others like himself. In his accelerated math class in which there is cross-age grouping of fourth to sixth grade high achievers in math, his teachers report that he gets along well with the other students.

SOCIALIZATION OF THE GIFTED

One major fear concerning gifted individuals who have great talent and seek perfection is that they may wind up isolated from others. Predictions of isolation were made early on by Alger (1867):

> A passion for perfection will make it a subject solitary as nothing else can. At every step he leaves a group behind. And, when at last, he reaches the goal, alas! Where are the early comrades? (p. 144)

Socialization Is an Educational Concern for the Gifted

Socialization continues to be a concern for gifted students; for example, one major reason gifted students are infrequently accelerated is the fear their social adjustment may be negatively affected. Yet, the research indicates gifted students have excellent social adjustment (Janos & Robinson, 1985; Robinson & Noble, 1991; Neihart, Reis, Robinson, & Moon, 2002; Colangelo, Assouline, & Gross, 2004). However, Silverman (1993b) said her clinical experience revealed that many of these so-called well-adjusted young gifted people suffer great loneliness and inner conflict between a "desire to fit in and their ideals" (p. 291).

One problem with many of the research studies on social adjustment is that gifted students have been compared to nongifted students, and the vulnerability of gifted students may not be reflected in these studies. Elizabeth Maxwell, the associate director of the Gifted Child Center in Denver, Colorado, said when there is a misfit between the gifted student and a given group, the gifted student often receives feedback that he or she does not fit, that he or she needs to change, and "that it is not all right to be oneself" (Genshaft, Bireley, & Hollinger, 1995, p. 27).

Socialization as a Level II Behavior in the Dabrowski Theory

In Level II of the Dabrowski Theory of Emotional Development, the individual is responsive to peers and a desire for approval exists. Individuals at this level are guided by custom and the expectations of others. Level II mirrors the definition of socialization as seeking to acquire the beliefs, behaviors, and values of others. In Level III there is a growing independence from social opinion, and discontent and disapproval of self. Gifted children want to be accepted and to be like others, and it is this desire to be like others that can be problematic for them, in that they are perceptive enough to know they are not like others, and this perception can be very troubling. This struggle is reflected in a journal entry of Shannon (age 16):

> I try so hard to be "with it" and to laugh at jokes I don't think are funny, and to act like I don't have one worry at all—but that's not me. I don't know who I am, and I am losing touch with myself.

This struggle to be like others and to take on the values and beliefs of the group can result in gifted students feeling alienated from themselves, and a loss of the essence of their inner self.

Social Development at Levels IV–V of the Dabrowski Theory

In Level IV of the Dabrowski Theory of Emotional Development, the individual begins to be objective, to step back, and to self-evaluate. Awareness of being unique grows, and one begins to design individual methods and strategies to deal with stress, anxiety, conflict, and depression. In Level V, the individual identifies with the highest levels of development and becomes autonomous, and at this level such individuals assume responsibility for others, as well as for their own development.

Social development is much broader than socialization and goes far beyond being aware of socially acceptable behavior. Social development involves the development of positive relationships with others that are symbiotic, as well as a deep concern for humanity.

Seeking Social Development Through Shared Experiences

Ruf (2005) said in *Losing Our Minds* that the key for good social interaction, friendships, and relationships to develop was for parents to arrange activities in which their gifted child could spend time with others with similar talents and abilities. In these social situations, gifted children can learn social skills as they interact with others who "get their jokes and share many of the same interests and abilities" (p. 305).

In the classroom and in social situations in which gifted students like Michael use vocabulary and humor that goes over the heads of the other children, they often have to choose to "pull back" or "shut down" to be able to maintain their integrity, or as Michael says, "to be me." One major benefit of placing Michael and other gifted students in a program for gifted students, whether it be a special class, or a cluster arrangement with several gifted students placed in one class, is the positive feedback they receive from one another, that they are "OK" and it is alright to be who they are.

Socialization Can Mask Giftedness

Gifted girls often fit in more easily than gifted boys because they perceive subtle social cues and respond accordingly (Reis, 1987). In the following interchange between a group of adolescents, Sara demonstrates her socialization skills; but unfortunately, she was not recommended for the district gifted program because her giftedness was masked by her socialization.

CASE STUDY

Mr. Lane enters the Science Class lab, immediately goes to the front of the room, and asks for volunteers to set up the lab. Sara raises her hand, along with Janelle, and both girls are given the handouts and materials to set up the lab. The students work in pairs, and later Mr. Lane asks for the students to share their findings. Sara pokes her lab partner Ty, and says, "Tell about our experiment." Ty raises his hand, and explains the methodology and results of their experiment, neglecting to share that Sara had the original idea. Mr. Lane praises Ty for his work and presentation. At the end of the class, Mr. Lane begins to pick up the lab materials, and Sara and Janelle bring the materials from their lab partners forward to the supply closet. Then they pick up several packets left behind by other students. Mr. Lane thanks the girls for their help.

Sara is a product of early conditioning concerning the importance of being helpful, and because of her social adaptation, her giftedness has not been noted, and in actuality her social adaptation may be hindering the full development of her talent. Kerr (1985) in studies on the developmental patterns of young gifted girls reported that gifted girls can be described as "social geniuses." According to Kerr, the problem with being a social genius is gifted girls may be taking a backseat intellectually, viewing themselves as a follower, rather than a leader. Sara says she hides her ability because she fears the other kids won't like her, which is representative of Level III conformative group thinking in the Dabrowski Theory of Emotional Development.

The socialization process of being a "helper" and a "good team player" can undermine the aspirations of gifted girls like Sara, and can insidiously affect their self-confidence. Reis (1987) found in her studies that women often focus their abilities on nurturing others, and seek careers in teaching and parenting—goals that preclude aiming for eminence.

HELP FOR DEVELOPING SOCIAL DEVELOPMENT

Opportunities to Explore Who They Are

Gifted adolescents, like all adolescents, are striving to find out who they are, and to which groups they belong, what talents and potential they have, and most importantly for gifted students, how can they contribute and how can they make a difference. This striving is reflected in a response to Question 19 on the Overexcitability Questionnaire: If you ask yourself "Who am I," what is the answer?

> That is a very big question. I often think of Popeye's saying, "I am what I am." I guess what I do is what I am, so here is a short list: I strive academically and continuously to further my knowledge, and I like to observe different people and their habits, and I enjoy teaching what I know, to share with others, and mainly I want to make a difference. I want my life to have mattered. I have this poster on my wall—LIVING MEANS PERPETUALLY SEARCHING FOR MEANING—and I really believe that! (John, age 18)

Making Assignments Relevant

Another idea that can be used to help gifted students explore who they are and help make assignments relevant is an Experience Wheel with which students compare their experience with those of fictional characters. Intrador (2005) shared how an English teacher designed an assignment for students to compare Huckleberry Finn's developmental journey with their own journey to adulthood. One student wrote:

> I like the story about Huck, but what I found more interesting was how this assignment made me think about my own journey. I'm not heading down the Mississippi, but connecting each stage of life that Huck experienced with my own helped me think about my own journey as well. (p. 24)

Boundary Breaking

In this collaborative activity, students are asked one question, and each student responds intuitively. Responses are usually given with the students taking turns, one after another if they are seated in a circle, or by rows or by tables. No comments are made while any one student is responding, only thoughtful reflection. At the end of a session, the teacher can ask what observations were made; for example, how are we alike and in what ways are we different? Boundary breaking questions can be as simple as, "If you could be an animal, what animal would you be?" Or more complex, such as, "If you could change one thing in the world, what would you change?"

At first, students may need to be reminded of the ground rules of boundary breaking, but they quickly internalize the underlying structure and protect the mutual acceptance, understanding, and trust that can be experienced in the activity. In boundary breaking, gifted students are provided opportunities to freely express feelings without judgment or comment. This activity helps gifted students experience a sense of dignity and worth, which counterbalances any previous negative experiences (Sisk, 1987).

Nell Noddings (2003) in *Happiness and Education* said if you are going to be a believer, you ought to be an intelligent believer, and know what it is you accept, and if possible why you accept it. Activities that are open-ended like boundary breaking can help gifted students explore who they are, and where they are going on their journey.

STRATEGIES TO BUILD POSITIVE SOCIAL DEVELOPMENT

Bibliotherapy

A favorite strategy for building social development is bibliotherapy; however, many teachers are reluctant to use this strategy for fear that it takes too much class time. In fact, a bibliotherapy session can last for as little as 15 to 20 minutes, and can involve a group of seven to fifteen students. The ideal group size for free and open discussion is seven to ten students, which provides time for a full exchange of ideas.

When a group of students have read a given story or book, they can make an appointment with the teacher, guidance counselor, librarian, or parent volunteer to participate in a bibliotherapy session. An example of an appointment sheet is depicted in Table 2.1.

The schedule in Table 2.1 indicates that two students have organized and encouraged seven students to discuss Tolan's book, *Surviving the Applewhites* (2003), and eleven students to discuss Avi's book, *Crispin: The Cross of Lead* (2002). The Pre-Advanced Placement English teacher will provide time for the students to conduct a bibliotherapy session, while the rest of the class is engaged in other small group work. In the bibliotherapy session, the teacher will use questions to explore a variety of types of thinking. An example of questions for *Surviving the Applewhites* by Stephanie Tolan includes questions framed around the Taylor Totem Pole: Academic, Planning, Predicting and Forecasting, Creative, and Decision Making (Taylor, 1963). After the students have had opportunities to participate in bibliotherapy, then they can construct their own questions; for example, the student leaders who organized the group of students for a bibliotherapy session could take this responsibility.

Students as young as third and fourth grade can successfully be involved in bibliotherapy sessions in which they also create the discussion questions. Upper elementary students can create questions for bibliotherapy sessions for younger students, and then visit those classes to lead sessions with the students. This type of collaborative activity demonstrates Level IV behavior of Dabrowski of reaching out to others, being of service, and assuming responsibility. An example of a bibliotherapy planning sheet with four questions addressing each of the five levels of the Taylor Totem Pole is included in Figure 2.1.

Bibliotherapy provides opportunities for wide exploration of books and stories, and stimulates further social development of gifted students; particularly, as they discuss the inner conflicts between the desires of the characters to fit in, or reaching for what Dabrowski calls one's ideals or higher self. In Tolan's book, *Surviving the Applewhites*, Jake makes tremendous strides toward a higher self, but so do most of the characters. Each of the characters has a certain vulnerability that gifted children can identify with, and they can vicariously learn from the experiences of the characters.

Table 2.1   Bibliotherapy Appointments

	Monday	*Tuesday*	*Wednesday*	*Thursday*	*Friday*
Student Leader		Tamika (7)			John (11)
Book Title		Tolan: *Surviving the Applewhites*			Avi: *Crispin: The Cross of Lead*

Figure 2.1   Bibliotherapy Planning Sheet

Summary: Jake Semple is a scary kid. Word has it that he burned down his old school, and then was kicked out of every other school in his home state. Only weeks into September, the middle school in Traybridge, North Carolina, has thrown him out, too. Now there's only one place left that will take him—a home school run by the most outrageous, forgetful, chaotic, quarrelsome family one would ever meet. Each and every Applewhite is an artist, except E.D. the smart, scruffy girl with a deep longing for order and predictability. E.D. and Jake are nearly the same age, and they quickly pair in the family experiment in cooperative education. In this experience, Jake and E.D. learn the value of their special gifts, and the family is brought together in their production of *The Sound of Music*.

Questions

Academic

1. What is the Creative Academy, and why is Jake there?
2. Why did E.D. decide to use those initials for her name?
3. What was Sybil Jameson famous for, and why didn't she use the name Applewhite?
4. Why didn't the Creative Academy have a curriculum?

Planning

1. Jake and E.D. were grouped as a class. How did E.D. plan to organize their work in a project?
2. What did Cordelia plan to do in the *Sound of Music* production?
3. How did Mr. Applewhite plan to conduct "color blind casting" for the show?
4. How did the family plan to put on their own *Sound of Music* production?

Predicting and Forecasting

1. Jake begins to see "himself as disappearing"—do you think he will change?
2. Do you think Hal will ever come out of his room and interact with the family? Why or why not?
3. Randolph Applewhite called Jake's voice magnificent. Do you think he will be a success in the production for the community theater?
4. How does the play transform Jake? Will he stay changed?

Creative

1. Destiny wanted to have hair like Jake. How did he create that look?
2. How did Jake create a living metamorphosis for his project?
3. How can E.D. use her creativity to save the production?
4. What project would you create if you were in the Creative Academy?

Decision Making

1. Did the technical staff have reasons to quit? What do you think about their decision?
2. Do you think the family appreciated Govindaswami, especially for his decisions about food?
3. Why didn't Jake run away from the Applewhites? What kept him there?
4. Do you think E.D. finally realized her value to the family? If so, how?

Other strategies that can be used to build positive social development for gifted students include:

- Reading biographies of eminent people
- Group projects that focus on human behavior
- Journal and personal writing
- Mentors

Reading Biographies of Eminent People

Dabrowski formulated his Theory of Emotional Development by reading biographies of creative and eminent people. As he studied their lives, he noted the values they pursued, and their struggles with the same misunderstandings he experienced in his life. This type of research can be helpful for gifted students, for as they see how eminent people struggle, and how they overcome trials and tribulations, and succeed in shaping meaningful careers and lives for themselves, they can develop a "tool box" of strategies for building their own positive social development.

Group Projects That Focus on Human Behavior

Human behavior projects can serve as service projects for gifted students to identify issues and propose solutions. One project that was successfully planned and carried out by a group of gifted adolescents in a summer program evolved from a newspaper article focusing on depression in the elderly. The reporter interviewed a number of people living in a local retirement facility, who said they wanted more interaction with young people. The retirees shared feelings of depression and feeling "old." The students decided to create a musical for the retirees. They selected musical pieces from their jazz ensemble, musical production, and choral classes, to be culminated with one-on-one discussions with each student selecting a retiree to talk with concerning their former career and life.

The students planned a two-hour presentation, to be followed by an hour for interaction with the retirees. The activity was such a success that the residents asked them to return the following week, and were quite disappointed to find out the students had used their last weekend in the university program to come and visit—and they were now dispersed throughout the state of Texas to their individual schools and homes. On their student evaluation of the three-week residential program, the human behavior project was mentioned by more than 80 percent of the students as a "highlight" in the program. The human behavior project represents a Level IV–V activity on the Dabrowski multilevels of development, turning empathy and love into action.

Journals and Personal Writing

In our complex and changing world, many people have learned to hide their feelings, and gifted students mirror their significant adults, parents, and teachers, who also may be reluctant to share their emotions and feelings. The price gifted students pay for withholding their emotions is that others may never truly understand them. One way to encourage gifted students to share emotions and feelings is through the use of journals. One teacher of the gifted has her students tape a large manila envelope to the side of their desk to hold their journal sheets. The students have red tags or flags that they can display if a feeling, emotion, or event in their journal needs to be shared.

A gifted student noted in his journal:

> I was really upset today when I didn't get chosen for team leader. When you asked me to help you with the project organization, that helped the PAIN a little. Thanks for being understanding. I guess I don't always have to be first. Was that what you meant by not always "tooting my horn?"

In this journal entry, the student can share his feelings about not being chosen, and to note his positive feelings, and awareness of the thoughtfulness of the teacher. He can communicate not only his feelings, but his insight. Informal journal communication can help teachers to better understand the concerns of their gifted students, and journal entries represent concrete reflections of the personal growth and social development of the students.

Mentors

When an appropriate match is made between a mentor and a mentee, both receive great benefit from the mentor experience. However, one potential problem with mentor programs for gifted students is that the mentor needs to be able to relate to gifted students. Some mentor programs involve shadowing the mentors in their workplace, and this can be meaningful in assisting gifted students in making career choices. Principles that can be helpful for school districts in establishing a mentor program for gifted students include:

1. The mentor program should be involved in some type of learning.
2. Both the mentor and mentee should be involved to some degree in selecting one another.
3. The mentor program needs to be open-ended and continue to evolve as the mentee and mentor get to know one another.

A mentor program that has been in operation for gifted students since the early 1970s in Tampa, Florida, focuses on four techniques: (1) attending, (2) responding, (3) personalizing, and (4) initiating. The attending and responding of the mentors help convince the mentees of their personal worth, and through responding and personalizing the mentor convinces the mentee that he or she is being understood. In addition, through initiating or devising a plan of action for the mentee, a natural growth in trust and empathy is developed.

HEARTS AND MINDS OF GIFTED STUDENTS

As gifted students become aware of their talents, teachers, counselors, and parents can touch their hearts and minds in a positive manner. When gifted students have opportunities to build a sense of their value and worth as contributing members of society, they become engaged in determining how best to use their talents. Educators can gain the positive attention of gifted students by engaging them in their studies in meaningful ways, by guiding them to explore who they are, and by helping them recognize conflicts as healthy ways to build a sense of responsibility.

This phenomenon is captured in the following response to Question 9 of the Overexcitability Questionnaire: What do you like to concentrate on the most?

> I really like to concentrate on my future. I already know what I would like to do for a career, so today is the best time to start working toward that career. I really appreciate being able to work with my mentor, who is an engineer. He makes me feel that there are no "stupid questions" and that my ideas are worthwhile. We are building an electric car, and I'm learning so much about my future work as an electrical engineer. (Mark, age 16)

SUMMARY

In this chapter, socialization of the gifted was discussed as a concern in gifted education. One of the major reasons gifted students are infrequently accelerated is the fear that their social adjustment may be negatively affected. This fear is not substantiated by the research on social adjustment of the gifted. However, one problem with the research is that many of the studies compared gifted students with nongifted students. Silverman (1993a) disagreed with these findings, and based on her clinical experience, she reported gifted students suffer loneliness and inner conflict in a desire to fit in with other students.

A distinction was made between socialization as Level II in the Dabrowski levels of development; whereas, social development represents a higher level of IV–V. In Level II, the individual is responsive to peers, and there is a desire for approval and attempts are made to acquire the beliefs, behaviors, and values of others. In Level III, the individual is stepping back and self-evaluating. In Level IV–V, the individual identifies with being autonomous and assumes responsibility for others. Social development involves the development of relationships with others and a deep concern for humanity.

Ruf (2005) stressed that the key for good social interaction was for parents to arrange activities in which their gifted child could spend time with others with similar talents and abilities. Socialization can mask giftedness, and a case study was examined to illustrate how the socialization process of being a "helper" can negatively affect the aspirations and the self-confidence of gifted girls. Reis (1987) found in her studies that women often focus their abilities on nurturing others and on careers in teaching and parenting, goals that she said preclude aiming for eminence.

Help for social development of gifted students was provided, including opportunities to explore who they are, making assignments relevant, and specific strategies like boundary breaking and bibliotherapy. A sample bibliotherapy planning sheet was provided based on the Taylor Creative Talent Model (Taylor, 1963). In addition, four strategies for building positive social development were discussed: (1) reading biographies of eminent people, (2) group projects that focus on human behavior, (3) journals and personal writing, and (4) mentors.

It was stressed that education can gain the hearts and minds of gifted students by engaging them in their studies in meaningful ways, by helping them to explore who they are, and by helping them to recognize conflicts as healthy ways to build a sense of responsibility.

Teacher Voice

This chapter opened my eyes to the struggle gifted students have in socialization. I never realized having an internal struggle to be socially accepted was an issue. I do understand the need to be accepted and fit in. Since second grade, I was in Challenge classes, attended a middle school with a special program for the gifted, and in high school, all my classes were pre-AP and AP. Growing up, I was always surrounded by other gifted kids, so I never had a strong, continuous internal conflict to fit in. I do remember though, my freshman year in high school, feeling slightly out of place. Transitioning from that special program in middle school to high school was hard because I wasn't completely surrounded by the same creative and gifted individuals. I held back many thoughts and opinions because I was a freshman in many sophomore classes. I didn't want to be the different smart girl; I just wanted to be normal.

Now as a teacher, I can use my own background and apply it toward helping my gifted students. I agree that parents and teachers can help the gifted child's social development. This chapter gave me ideas for fostering social development in my classroom. I am going to have my fourth graders share some of their creative activities and products with second or third graders. I think my gifted students would enjoy this, but they would also benefit from the experience.

A teacher's classroom should be a safe, positive environment for all students. In my class, no question is stupid, and all of my students are always working in groups.

Amy Graham
Fourth grade teacher

Read On

Intrador, S. (2005). The engaging classroom. *Educational Leadership, 62*(1), 20–24.

Perkins, D. (2005). Knowledge alive. *Educational Leadership, 62*(1), 16–18.

Pope, D. C. (2001). *Doing school: How we are creating a generation of stressed and materialistic and miseducated students.* New Haven, CT: Yale University Press.

Silverman, L. (1995). The universal experience of being out of sync. In L. K. Silverman (Ed.), *Advanced development: A collection of works on gifted adults* (pp. 1–12). Denver, CO: Institute for the Study of Advanced Development.

Log On

Association for Experiential Education (http://www.aee.org/). A Web site with resources to make direct hands-on experiences in teaching.

Educators for Social Responsibility (http://www.esrnational.org/). Provides tools for planning student projects on conflict resolution and understanding world cultures.

Edutopia Online (http://www.edutopia.org/projectbasedlearning/). A George Lucas Web site with information and resources to implement project-based learning.

Reflect On

- Reflect on the notion that when students find the right connections, they will learn—they won't be able to help themselves. When have you had that experience?
- The project-approach responds to the curiosity of children and makes project work generative and engaging. What types of projects have worked for you?
- Think about inner conflicts you may have had, and how you managed to redirect your energy in positive ways.

REFERENCES

Alger, W. K. (1867). *The solitudes of nature and man: Or the loneliness of human life.* Boston: Roberts Bros.

Avi. (2002). *Crispin: The cross of lead.* New York: Scholastic.

Colangelo, N. Assouline, S., & Gross, M. (2004). *A nation deceived: How schools hold back America's brightest students* (Vol. I). Iowa City: University of Iowa Press.

Genshaft, J., Bireley, M., & Hollinger, C. (1995). *Serving gifted and talented students: A resource for school personnel.* Austin, TX: Pro-ed.

Hollingworth, L. (1930). Personality development of special class children. University of Pennsylvania Bulletin. *Seventeenth Annual Schoolmen's Week Proceedings, 30,* 442–446.

Intrador, S. (2005). The engaging classroom. *Educational Leadership, 62*(1), 20–24.

Janos, P., & Robinson, N. M. (1985). Psychosocial development in intellectually gifted children. In F. D. Horowitz & M. O'Brien (Eds), *The gifted and talented: Developmental perspectives* (pp. 149–195). Washington, DC: American Psychological Association.

Kerr, B. (1985). *Smart girls, gifted women.* Columbus, OH: Psychology Press.

Neihart, M., Reis, S., Robinson, N., & Moon, S. (2002). *The social and emotional development of gifted children*. Waco, TX: Prufrock Press.

Noddings, N. (2003). *Happiness and education*. Cambridge: Cambridge University Press.

Perkins, D. (2005). Knowledge alive. *Educational Leadership, 62*(1), 16–18.

Pope, D. C. (2001). *Doing school: How we are creating a generation of stressed and materialistic and miseducated students*. New Haven, CT: Yale University Press.

Reis, S. (1987). We can't change what we don't recognize: Understanding the special needs of gifted females. *Gifted Child Quarterly, 31*, 83–89.

Robinson, N., & Noble, K. D. (1991). Socio-emotional development and adjustment of gifted children. In M. C. Wang, M. C. Reynolds, & H. J. Walberg (Eds.), *Handbook of special education: Research and practice* (Vol. IV), (pp. 57–76). New York: Pergamon Press.

Ruf, D. (2005). *Losing our minds*. Scottsdale, AZ: Great Potential Press.

Silverman, L. (1993a). The gifted individual. In L. K. Silverman (Ed.), *Counseling the gifted and talented* (pp. 3–28). Denver, CO: Love.

Silverman, L. (1993b). Social development, leadership and gender. In L. K. Silverman (Ed.), *Counseling the gifted and talented* (pp. 291–327). Denver, CO: Love.

Silverman, L. (1995). The universal experience of being out of sync. In L. K. Silverman (Ed.), *Advanced development: A collection of works on gifted adults* (pp. 1–12). Denver, CO: Institute for the Study of Advanced Development.

Sisk, D. (1987). *Creative teaching of the gifted*. New York: McGraw-Hill.

Taylor, C. (1963). Clues to creative teaching: The creative process and education. *Instructor, 73*, 4–5.

Terman, L. (1931). The gifted child. In C. Murchinson (Ed.) *A handbook of child psychology* (pp. 568–584). Worcester, MA: Clark University Press.

Terrassier, J. (1985). Dyssynchrony: Uneven development. In J. Freeman (Ed.) *The psychology of gifted children* (pp. 265–274). New York: John Wiley.

Tolan, S. (2003). *Surviving the Applewhites*. New York: Scholastic.

3

Perfectionism

A Positive or Negative Characteristic of Giftedness?

Elizabeth listens to the sounds in her house to make sure she can quietly go back to her computer without waking her parents and continue to work on an assignment that is due tomorrow. She reads what she has written, rewords it, and then edits it one more time. This has been going on all afternoon and evening, until her mother insisted she go to bed. Elizabeth muses, "Why can't I just turn this paper in like all my friends?" And she answers herself, "Because I don't want it to be just good; I want it to be excellent." With this thought in mind, she rereads the paper one more time.

Elizabeth's mother says it is hard to live with her perfectionism, and even harder to watch her daughter's frustration and emotional intensity when she insists she can't have errors in her work. As a young child, Elizabeth was upset when her coloring wasn't just right and would tear up her papers and start over again. In school, she would smash the clay figures because the shape she was forming did not match her mental image, or as she said, the "sculpture in my mind."

In this chapter, we examine the passion for perfectionism in gifted children and adults, as well as the research that indicates there is a healthy perfectionism. The distinction between perfectionism and the pursuit of excellence is discussed, along with Silverman's (1999) six reasons why gifted students are perfectionists. Techniques to help gifted students explore their attitude about perfectionism are examined, and a case study of middle school perfectionists and their counselor demonstrates group discussion and reflection as tools of understanding for gifted students.

A section on "Help for Perfectionists" includes modeling and affirmations by teachers, counselors, and parents; curriculum materials that encourage mastery; and open-ended assignments. In addition, project learning is discussed as a strategy to provide perfectionists choice, challenge, creativity, and real-life application. This chapter's final focus is on the need for gifted students to develop self-regulation. Their need to develop reasoning, resilience, and responsibility are addressed in the Other 3Rs Project. Gifted students work best when their intrinsic motivation is engaged, and this is illustrated with exemplary teaching activities.

PASSION FOR PERFECTION

A passion for perfection is one of the characteristics of gifted children and adults, and no doubt one of the most misunderstood aspects of giftedness. Perfectionism tends to be misunderstood by those who counsel the gifted, whether by parents—as in the case of Elizabeth's mother, who insisted she stop working and go to bed—or by teachers and counselors who view perfectionism as a negative trait. Dabrowski & Piechowski (1977) described perfectionism as a drive for self-perfection, or a dissatisfaction with "what is" and a yearning for what "ought to be." Silverman (1999) stressed that perfectionism is the hallmark of giftedness, and I would add the pain of perfectionistic efforts is part of being gifted. Perfectionism is a formidable force capable of bringing not only intense pain, frustration, and mental paralysis, but it can also bring tremendous satisfaction and creative contribution, depending upon how it is channeled.

Perfectionists are capable of incredible highs, and of being totally involved in what the psychologist Csikszentmihaly (1990) called *flow*. He describes this phenomenon:

> The best moments usually occur when a person's body or mind is stretched to its limits in a voluntary effort to accomplish something difficult and worthwhile. Optimum experience is thus something that we can make happen; . . . such experiences are not necessarily pleasant at the time they occur. The swimmer's muscles might have ached during his most memorable race, his lungs might have felt like exploding, and he might have been dizzy with fatigue—yet these could have been the best moments of his life. (pp. 5–6)

Perfectionism as an energy can incapacitate and cause a type of mental paralysis in which the individual can't or won't start a project, thinking that the task is impossible. On the other hand, perfectionism can provide energy leading one to struggle and achieve outstanding creative works of art, music, literature, and, according to Maslow (1954), a "fine soup."

What Does Research Say About Perfectionism?

Hamachek (1978) proposed a concept of perfectionism allowing for a healthy form of perfectionism. He divided perfectionists into people who derive pleasure from completing difficult tasks and neurotic perfectionists who never feel what they accomplish is good enough. Hamachek developed a scale including (1) concern over making mistakes, (2) high personal standards, (3) perception of high parental criticism, (4) doubting the quality of one's actions, and (5) high preference for order and organization.

Healthy Perfectionists and Dysfunctional Perfectionists

Schuler (1994) developed a *Goals and Work Habits Survey* and normed the instrument with 336 gifted adolescents nationwide, including a broad base of racial, social, and economic levels. Then she conducted a study of gifted adolescents in a rural setting and found both healthy and dysfunctional perfectionists. Healthy perfectionists had a strong need for organization and order, accepted that they made mistakes, and enjoyed the fact that their parents held high expectations for them. They reported positive ways of coping with perfectionism, had adults who modeled doing their best, and viewed effort as an important part of their perfectionism. Dysfunctional perfectionists were anxious about making mistakes, held extremely high standards for themselves, perceived that others held excessive standards for them, internalized negative remarks from others, questioned their own judgments, lacked effective coping strategies, and exhibited a constant need for approval.

The majority of the gifted students in Schuler's study reported little or no contact with the counselors in their schools. Several students listed a program called Study Buddy and an advisory group, but most of the students described the work of the counselor as involving serious problems, which could indicate that the students didn't see perfectionism as serious, or that their counselors didn't view it as serious. Schuler shared advice suggested by students in her study:

> Well, people who are perfectionists usually get worried very easily. So if they were taught a couple of methods to use for anxiety, that might help a little bit. Teach relaxation techniques in elementary school. Just be there . . . for whenever anybody might need you. And just remember that. And comfort, because everybody doesn't have to be perfect all the time. (Schuler, 1999, p. 91)

One useful distinction for understanding perfectionism is the concept of a perfectionist as someone who thinks anything short of perfection in performance is unacceptable; whereas, the person who strives for excellence can feel great personal satisfaction and pride in a good-enough performance (Adderholdt-Elliott, 1978). Individuals who strive for excellence have good self-esteem and want to do well to master a task, and they challenge themselves to know as much as possible and to be the best.

Perfectionism and the Pursuit of Excellence

In the book *Perfectionism*, Adderholdt-Elliott (1978) stressed that people who pursue excellence are hard workers and are confident. They feel good about a score of 96, and they are willing to try new ways of doing things, to take risks, and to learn from their mistakes. On the other hand, Adderholdt-Elliott said perfectionists overwork, don't feel confident, procrastinate, and feel like a failure if they don't receive 100. In addition, perfectionists prefer to work alone because they feel others will not do a good job, and this will affect their final product and grade. With all of the current emphasis in education on cooperative learning, a preference for working alone can be problematic for gifted students.

Six Reasons Gifted Children Are Perfectionists

Silverman (1999) listed six reasons why gifted children are perfectionists. First, perfection is an abstract concept, and it takes an abstract mind to grasp its meaning and to cherish a vision that does not exist in the concrete world. Second, perfectionism is a function of asynchrony or uneven development. Third, many gifted children have older playmates, so they tend to set standards appropriate for their more mature friends. Fourth, young gifted children have enough forethought to enable them to be successful in their first attempts at mastering any skill. Fifth, the gifted crave challenge and stimulation, and if school work is too easy, they will do whatever they can to complicate the task, including trying to accomplish it perfectly. Sixth, perfectionism occurs as a distortion of the drive for self-perfection, which is a positive evolutionary drive.

Emily (aged 15) a healthy perfectionist shares the following:

> My school doesn't have a gifted program, so when the teachers give an assignment, I think what else could I do to make this more interesting and worthwhile pursuing—I just sort of shape my own study. Sometimes I add graphs, sometimes I do small studies with my family or friends to illustrate a point. Trust me, not all of my teachers like this addition to their assignment—but I say so what; I'll do it my way.

GROUP DISCUSSION AND REFLECTION AS TECHNIQUES TO HELP GIFTED STUDENTS EXPLORE ATTITUDES ABOUT PERFECTION

Twelve gifted students were invited to a group discussion to discuss the topic "To Be Nobody but Myself." The students were provided with the following quotation from e.e. cummings: "To be nobody but myself—in a world that is doing its best, night and day, to make you everybody else—means to fight the hardest battle which any human being can fight, and never stop fighting." The students were asked to volunteer to spend an half hour with the counselor in their middle school to discuss perfectionism in an effort to see if discussion groups involving attitude exploration could be helpful for the students and the counselors. Their Pre-Advanced Placement Science teacher asked students who felt they were perfectionists to raise their hand, then said that the counselor needed volunteers for a discussion group. Seven girls and five boys volunteered for the group.

CASE STUDY

Miss Elliot, a middle school counselor, was sitting in a circle of twelve chairs arranged in the front of the Pre-AP Science lab. She passed a quotation from e.e. cummings to the group of students, and asked them to read it, and to share any connections they could make to perfectionism. She indicated they would be using a "talking stick," which they could pass around when they wished to make a comment, to encourage full participation.

One student, Paul, reached for the talking stick and said, "Trying to be like everyone else means being, as they say, on the same page, and I don't want to be on the same page. I want to be on my page." The counselor nodded and asked Paul, "What does that mean, my page?"

Paul replied, "Like in the science class, we have to identify a project, and carry it out, but it was so spelled out, that the projects will all be the same, with the same results, the same amount of time, and the same everything. What is different about that?" Another student, Martha asked for the talking stick, and added, "It's not only the science class, but in most of my classes, if you want to do extra, or be different, it is discouraged; plus, my parents won't let me stay up and work on my projects past 11 PM, and I am always late anyway. I need more time if it is going to be my best work."

Elizabeth, leaned over and took the stick from Martha. "I can't get started right away. It takes time for me to decide what I want to do, so I usually go along with others, and then if I don't try, I haven't lost anything." Paul responded to Elizabeth, "Yeah, I know how that is. You make a deal with yourself, like if I just get by, it's OK. But then I feel bad because it's not my best work. My dad is a perfectionist, and I guess my mom is too."

The counselor looked around the circle and then asked the students if most of their parents were perfectionists. Only three of the students agreed, but all of them identified

(Continued)

(Continued)

someone in their family who was a perfectionist, a grandmother, a brother, a sister, and an uncle. The counselor then asked, "What's good or bad about being a perfectionist?"

Jon observed, "It looks like all of us have someone who is a perfectionist, who probably acts like a role model. I get so worried about my projects and assignments that I feel sick to my stomach, and that is what's bad about perfectionism." At that point, most of the students began adding negative feelings and behaviors related to their perfectionism, including headaches, depression, eating junk food, and not sleeping. One student described a feeling of "having arms that weigh a ton."

The counselor waited until all of the students had a turn with the talking stick to share negative behaviors of perfectionism, then asked, "What do you do to handle your perfectionism?" and "Can perfectionism be good?" The group of students thought for a moment, and began making suggestions:

- Use humor and laugh at yourself when you get stuck.
- Make a schedule and try to stick to it.
- Make it OK to make mistakes, but learn from them.
- Take the dog for a walk.

The counselor listened to the suggestions, and then stepped to the board to list the suggestions for the group. "These are great suggestions," she said. "Let me add another: make a mental picture of having completed your project and think how great you would feel." One student replied, "I do that Miss Elliot, and it usually works, unless I have bitten off more than I can chew. And when I finish a good project, I feel great." Sue added, "Perfectionism works for me because I'm not satisfied with C work; I want A work. Then I am happy with myself."

"Then that is where you need to be realistic," said the counselor, "and that is difficult." She indicated that their half hour was up and asked if the discussion had been helpful for them. The students all agreed it was and asked if they could talk with her again. She asked them to reflect on: "What's the worst thing that could happen if you don't do something perfectly?" The students began to talk among themselves as they left the room, and the counselor could see they had been successfully involved in "attitude exploration" about perfectionism.

Miss Elliot met with the middle school teachers in their faculty meeting the next day to share what she and the students had experienced in the discussion group. The teachers identified additional strategies they could use with perfectionistic students to help them deal with the social and emotional issues of perfectionism.

One language arts teacher said, "I will talk to my group of students about their small group projects for next week about people who have achieved excellence, and I know many eminent people were perfectionists." The counselor suggested two more techniques, role playing and bibliotherapy, as strategies to deal with the emotional and social issues of perfectionism. At which point, another teacher added that her class was reading Linda Sue Park's book, *A Single Shard,* in which one of the characters is a perfectionist and eventually achieves an outstanding product. The teachers were enthusiastic and responsive in the discussion on perfectionism, and several indicated they were perfectionists.

HELPING PERFECTIONISTS

Modeling

Modeling and affirmations by teachers and parents can be helpful with young perfectionists, such as saying often and sincerely, "It doesn't matter that you make a mistake because everyone does. What matters is what you do with your mistake. One of the purposes of your good brain is to figure out what to do with your mistakes" (Hollingsworth, 1999, p. 441).

Curriculum Materials That Encourage Mastery

Curriculum materials that encourage and provide gifted students the freedom to achieve mastery and move on at their own pace can be helpful for perfectionists. One example of this type of curriculum is the Kumon Math program, which provides a standard completion time, as well as an acceptable number of mistakes. Many perfectionistic young children are fearful of making mistakes. As a result they proceed slowly through tasks and sometimes don't finish their work on time. Kumon is helpful for these youngsters because it gives them permission to make a reasonable number of mistakes.

Open-Ended Assignments

Another way to channel the perfectionism of gifted students is to provide opportunities for them to work on open-ended assignments. When gifted students identify the topic, establish the questions they want to explore, and design both the process and product, they develop a feeling of being "in control." Open-ended assignments lessen the perfectionistic negative self-talk about someone else making all the decisions on what to study.

Project-Based Learning

Project-based learning can provide the perfectionist opportunities for choice, challenge, creativity, and real-life application. When project-based learning is used with a group of students, each student can have a unique culminating project. Imagine a project assigned by Teacher A, who asks students to write a term paper on a specific topic and specifies that it be ten double-spaced pages, contain ten references, is due in three weeks, and must be done individually. Contrast that to Teacher B, who tells the students that the topic is unspecified, they can choose a topic of interest that they can work on individually or in pairs, and that they are to give a presentation in class, either a poster, PowerPoint, or group activity. Teacher B's assignment has more opportunity for self-regulation. The key for the perfectionist is "choice" in their studies.

DIMENSIONS OF SELF-REGULATION

The dimensions of self-regulation in which students have choice is reflected in the work of Zimmerman (2006) in a conceptual framework organized around six key learning questions. Self-regulation includes *why*, which involves setting goals and working toward self-efficacy, and *how*, by identifying and developing strategies for reaching the goals and using them often so they become routine. *When* involves time management, and *what* is the process of becoming more aware of one's accomplishments—it is stepping back and observing and evaluating oneself. *Where* is recognizing that not every place or environment is conducive to studying and finding the right place, and *with whom* includes the idea that some projects will involve other students or people as resources. The process shown in Table 3.1 can be self-regulated by students as in the following case study.

Table 3.1   Dimensions of Self-Regulation

Learning Questions	*Self-Regulating Processes*
Why?	Self-efficacy and self-goals
How?	Strategy use or routinized performance
When?	Time management
What?	Self-observation, self-judgment, self-reaction
Where?	Environmental structuring
With Whom?	Selective help-seeking

CASE STUDY

Megan, an eighth grade honors student, is working through the six key questions in her English project. The response to *why*: the paper is a requirement, and Megan has an A going into the assignment and would like to maintain that grade. Therefore, her goal is to submit a quality project worth an A. The *how* is to set time aside for a routinized study time. Megan decides to work every evening from 7 PM to 9 PM, and this also takes care of the *when* of time management. The *what* involves self-observation, self-judgment, and self-reaction. Megan keeps a journal, and she reads her previous journal response to a project for the same teacher:

> I don't know why I stew around so over the honors English project. I always get an A, but I want my paper to be one that Miss Lansing keeps as a model for other students. My biggest problem is thinking and thinking before I write.

Megan reflects on this journal entry, and decides that she will control the *where* with some environmental structuring and make sure there are no distractions from 7 PM to 9 PM. She decides to work with her friend Erin for *with whom* to share her ideas before she writes her paper. Megan reflects that Erin gets As in class and she always has good ideas. Plus, Megan chuckles, she is so positive that this may "rub off on me."

Students who are introduced to the six key questions of self-regulation can reflect on the importance of goal attainment and establish individual goals that they will value.

Self-Observation, Self-Judgment, and Self-Reaction

Self-regulation involves self-observation, self-judgment, and self-reaction. The perfectionist can keep track of the frequency, intensity, or quality of their perfectionistic behavior. Students having difficulty settling down to study can keep a written record of their activities, and they may find they are wasting a lot of time on nonacademic tasks or engaging in negative self-talk and anxiety about a task.

Strategies to Control Anxiety and Negative Self-talk

The following strategies can be helpful for perfectionistic students to use and to control their anxiety and negative self-talk.

- Count to ten in your head.
- Do deep and slow breathing while counting to ten.
- Distract yourself (sing or whistle to yourself).
- Visualize yourself having successfully completed the project and feel the emotion behind that success.
- Make a list of your strengths.
- Make a list of your available resources.
- Think about what would be the worst thing that could happen if you don't complete the task on time.
- Think of ways to make sure you do complete the task.

These strategies also can help perfectionistic students to use and to control their emotions involved in their perfectionism.

OTHER 3Rs PROJECT (REASONING, RESILIENCE, AND RESPONSIBILITY)

Another useful activity to help perfectionists cope is the Other 3Rs Project. This project focuses on reasoning, resilience, and responsibility. The 3Rs can be stressed with perfectionistic students, and teachers and counselors can tell them that research shows reasoning, resilience, and responsibility are related to student success, which is one of the important motivators for the perfectionists—they want to succeed. Cogan and Subotnik (2006) stressed that reasoning offers students a number of strategies to solve problems, that resilience helps students focus on overcoming learning obstacles rather than feeling despair over failure, and that skills of responsibility help them take charge of their achievement through effort and self-regulation. They also suggested that the following ideas be presented to students concerning reasoning, resilience, and responsibility.

Reasoning

What strategies would help me solve the problem?

Resilience

Challenges are normal. We all have them.

What can I learn from this stumbling block or setback?

How can I approach this challenge in a different way?

Responsibility

It's up to me to create the results I want.

How I act matters.

I will listen and care about what you have to say.

I care about what is good for all of us, not just for me.

I will help if you want or need it.

I'm glad I can ask you for help. (p. 18)

INTRINSIC MOTIVATION

Perfectionists work best when they engage their intrinsic motivation. Schunk, Pintrich, and Meece (2008) list four sources of intrinsic motivation: challenge, curiosity, control, and fantasy. These are illustrated in Table 3.2 with exemplary teaching activities.

Table 3.2   Intrinsic Motivators and Activities

Intrinsic Motivators	Activities
Challenge	Students engage in tasks of intermediate difficulty that they feel they can accomplish
Curiosity	Students are presented surprising/incongruous information to motivate them to fill a gap in their knowledge
Control	Students are provided choice and a sense of control over their learning
Fantasy	Students work with fantasy and make-believe in simulations and games

Using Intrinsic Motivators in Simulation Games

Simulation games provide gifted students opportunities to be involved in intrinsically motivating activities that address *challenge*, as students engage in tasks that tap their *curiosity*. Players are provided choice and they feel a sense of *control*, and most simulations involve *fantasy* or make-believe situations. An example of a simulation in action called *Land of the Sphinx and Land of the Rainbow* (Sisk, 1983) illustrates the use of the four intrinsic motivators.

The setting for the game is the year 2050, and a minimum of four students are selected to role-play travelers who visit the two lands: Land of the Sphinx and Land of the Rainbow. The remaining students are randomly selected by counting off by 1 and 2. The 1s are assigned to live in the Land of the Sphinx and the 2s to live in the Land of the Rainbow. Each group of students is provided a scenario or script for them to use in completing three tasks that match the description of their land: (1) design an education program, (2) plan a research project, and (3) create a policy statement about the environment. The scenarios for the Land of the Sphinx describe it as a land inhabited by people who trust logic, objectivity, and implicit action. Order is very important to them, particularly schedules, rules, and routine. The Land of the Rainbow is described as inhabited by people interested in a deeper, larger, all-embracing reality, and they follow their hunches. They are creative and love music and art. Students in one land do not have the description or scenario of the people in the other land.

The four travelers are asked to visit the two lands and to find out as much information as they can by asking questions with enthusiasm and curiosity (the travelers do not have copies of the scenarios of the two lands). They are told to be bold, open, and courageous; to decide which land they would want to live in; and to make a list of their reasons for selecting that land.

Each group of students in the two lands is provided 30 minutes to design an educational program, a research project, and an environmental policy. During that half hour, the travelers can plan the questions they will ask the students in each land, which further stimulates their curiosity to find out about the two lands.

The depth and breadth of creativity demonstrated by the students will vary with the age of the group playing the game. One group of middle school students who role-played living in the Land of the Rainbow designed an educational system that was essentially homeschooling, in which all of the citizens taught the children using a curriculum based on the interests of the children. There were no grades, only the satisfaction of the children was to be measured. They paraphrased a song for their land that focused on *Stand by Me for Creativity*, which became their motto. When the travelers visited their land, all of the citizens embraced them, and offered snacks that they said were grown organically on their farms. Their research project was to measure the effect of organic foods on the "satis-faction" of the children homeschooled by the community. Their policy concerning the environment was simply "We love and protect our land." Their leader served for one year, and was selected by majority vote, with each member having one vote.

The students in the Land of the Sphinx developed an educational system based on tests, in which students who could pass a test could go on to the next grade. Everyone was required to go to college. Their research project involved protecting the environment, and they had fines for pollution and the overuse of water. Cars that were more than ten years old were confiscated by the king of the Land of the Sphinx and scrapped. Visitors were required to make appointments with the king's advisor and to put their questions in writing. Visitations were on Mondays and Fridays, and limited to one half-hour.

This simulation game usually takes one class period. In the debriefing, the teacher can ask the travelers to indicate which land they would select as their home. It is not uncommon for the travelers to select neither land. One traveler said, "The Land of the Rainbow was just too unstructured and different for me." Another traveler said, "The Land of the Sphinx was too strict and rigid—there were too many rules." Instead, the four travelers described a land that combined the best of both lands.

In the debriefing, the teacher will need to encourage the gifted students to identify and to discuss real-life situations similar to those simulated in the game. The teacher of the middle school students asked his students to talk about what might be done when someone is placed in a situation in which he or she does not know the rules of a new culture. The teacher also asked if any students were uncomfortable in their land: "Was it too open or too rigid?" Again, the individual preferences of the students helped the teacher to gain valuable insight about his student's preferences. One student spontaneously summarized the activity thusly: "It's like honoring both sides of the brain: the Rainbow is the creative right and the Sphinx is the logical left. Am I right?" The teacher then addressed stereotyping and cultural bias, as well as the importance of adaptation and accommodation.

SUMMARY

This chapter examined the passion for perfectionism of gifted children and adults. Research indicates that there is a healthy form of perfectionism, and Hamachek (1978) developed a scale to measure perfectionism that included concern over making mistakes, high personal standards, perception of high parental criticism, doubting the quality of one's actions, and high preference for order and organization. Schuler (1999) conducted a national research study with gifted adolescents and identified healthy perfectionists and dysfunctional perfectionists.

A useful distinction was made between perfectionism and the pursuit of excellence by Adderholdt-Elliott (1978), who said people who pursue excellence are hard workers and confident, whereas perfectionists overwork, don't feel confident, procrastinate, and feel like a failure if they don't receive an A. Silverman's six reasons why gifted students are perfectionists were presented: (1) perfectionism is an abstract concept, and it takes an abstract mind to grasp its meaning; (2) perfectionism is a function of asynchrony or uneven development; (3) many gifted children have older playmates, so they tend to set standards appropriate for their more mature friends; (4) young gifted children have enough forethought to enable them to be successful in their first attempts at mastering any skill; (5) the gifted crave challenge and stimulation, and if school work is too easy, they will do whatever they can to complicate the task, including trying to accomplish it perfectly; and (6) perfectionism occurs as a distortion of the drive for self-perfection, which is a positive evolutionary drive (Silverman, 1999).

Group discussion and reflection were discussed as techniques to help gifted students explore attitudes about perfectionism through a case study of twelve middle school perfectionists and their counselor. A section on "Help for Perfectionists" included the use of modeling and affirmations by teachers and parents, curriculum materials that encourage mastery, and open-ended assignments.

In addition, project-based learning was discussed as a strategy to provide perfectionists an opportunity for choice, challenge, creativity, and real-life application. The dimensions of self-regulation in which learners have choice was explored, using the self-regulation processes of Zimmerman (2006). Six learning questions and self-regulating processes involving self-observation, self-judgment, and self-reaction were discussed as being helpful to the perfectionist. Anxiety and negative self-talk can be problems for students with perfectionism, and strategies were listed that can assist gifted students in learning how to control their emotions involved in perfectionism. The Other 3Rs Project of Cogan, Sternberg, and Subotnik (2006) was discussed as a means to focus on reasoning, resilience, and responsibility.

Perfectionists work best when they engage their intrinsic motivation, and the four intrinsic motivators as outlined by Schunk, Pintrich, and Meece (2008) were illustrated, with exemplary teaching activities, using simulation games. The importance of processing a simulation was stressed because in analyzing their experiences in simulations, gifted students can capitalize on the full learning potential of the strategy. Gifted students learn and remember best when they fully participate in the debriefing, and they naturally move toward summarizing, generalizing, and identifying the big idea of the simulation game. In the debriefing, one middle school student said, "It's like honoring both sides of the brain: the Rainbow is the creative right and the Sphinx is the logical left. Am I right?"

The next chapter addresses the need for gifted students to develop moral courage and identifies ways gifted students can learn to live deeply with immutable values. The focus is on learning how to dare to try different things and how to find the strength to follow through.

Teacher Voice

I tend to view perfectionism in a student as positive or negative, depending on how it affects him or her in my classroom. Perfectionists are driven by an inner force to explore beyond assignments. Their motives are often misconstrued as attempts to please the teacher, when in reality the person perfectionists are most interested in pleasing is themselves. The grade may not be as important to them as the discovery process and the final outcome. This inner drive of perfectionists can be viewed as positive when it pushes them to success that is seemingly beneficial both to themselves and society. I don't doubt that there are many moments of self-satisfaction, but I often wonder at what cost these students contribute to society. Parents and teachers need to bring balance to help them set high but attainable goals without the stress and frustration of perfectionism. When one sets out on a journey, getting lost can either be one's worst nightmare or one's best adventure, depending on one's perspective. We need to help perfectionists keep their tasks in proper perspective and learn to enjoy the journey.

Carolyn Barnes
Middle school teacher

Read On

Cogan, J., Sternberg, R, & Subotnik, R. (2006). Integrating the other 3 Rs into the school curriculum. In R. J. Sternberg & R. F. Subotnik (Eds.), *Optimizing student success with the other three Rs* (pp. 227–240). Greenwich, CT: Information Age.

Schuler, P. (2002). Perfectionism in gifted children and adolescents. In M. Neihart, S. Reis, N. Robinson, & S. Moon (Eds), *The social and emotional development of gifted children* (pp. 71–81). Waco, TX: Prufrock Press.

Schuler, P., & Siegle, D. (2000). Perfectionism differences in gifted middle school students. *Roeper Review, 23,* 39–44.

Silverman, L. (1993). The gifted individual. In L. K. Silverman (Ed.), *Counseling the gifted and talented* (pp. 3–28). Denver, CO: Love.

Silverman, L. (1998). Through the lens of giftedness. *Roeper Review, 20,* 204–210.

Log On

The Other 3Rs Project (http://www.apa.org/ed/cpse/threershome.html). Provides information on Project 3Rs (reasoning, responsibility, and resilience) and its integration into the curriculum.

Reflective Thought/Critical Thinking (http://www.ed.gov/databases/ERIC_Digests/ed436007.html). This site provides a number of research-based articles on reflective thought and critical thinking.

Who Did It? (http://school.discovery.com/lessonplans/programs/whodidit). A Web page to stimulate discovery.

Reflect On

- How important is "feeling good about yourself"?
- How often do you provide learners with choices and a sense of control over their learning outcomes?
- Perfectionists need to master intrinsic motivation that is realistic, and curiosity is a key to intrinsic motivation. Think of a lesson in which you presented students with surprising or incongruous information to motivate them to close a gap in their knowledge.

REFERENCES

Adderholdt-Elliott, M. R. (1978). *Perfectionism: What's bad about being too good?* Minneapolis, MN: Free Spirit.

Cogan, J., Sternberg, R., & Subotnik, R. (2006). Integrating the other 3 Rs into the school curriculum. In R. J. Sternberg & R. F. Subotnik (Eds.), *Optimizing student success with the other three Rs* (pp. 227–240). Greenwich, CT: Information Age.

Cogan, J., & Subotnik, R. (2006). Reasoning, resilience, & responsibility. *Understanding Our Gifted, 19*(1), 17–20.

Csikszentmihaly, M. (1990). *Flow: The psychology of optimal experience.* New York: Harper & Row.

Dabrowski, K., & Piechowski, M. (1977). *Theory of levels of emotional development* (Vols. 1 & 2). Oceanside, NY: Dabor Science.

Hamachek, D. E. (1978). Psychodynamics of normal and neurotic perfectionism. *Psychology, 15*, 27–33.

Hollingsworth, P. (1999). Open systems concepts. In J. Smutny (Ed.), *The young gifted child* (pp. 432–444). Cresskill, NJ: Hampton Press.

Maslow, A. (1954). *Motivation and personality.* New York: Harper & Row.

Schuler, P. (1994). *Goals and work habits survey.* Unpublished instrument. Storrs: University of Connecticut.

Schuler, P. (1999). *Voices of perfectionism: Perfectionistic gifted adolescents in a rural middle school.* Washington, DC: Department of Education.

Schuler, P. (2002). Perfectionism in gifted children and adolescents. In M. Neihart, S. Reis, N. Robinson, & S. Moon (Eds), *The social and emotional development of gifted children* (pp. 71–81). Waco, TX: Prufrock Press.

Schuler, P., & Siegle, D. (2000). Perfectionism differences in gifted middle school students. *Roeper Review, 23*, 39–44.

Schunk, D, Pintrich, P., & Meece, J. (2008). *Motivation in education: Theory, research and applications.* Columbus, OH: Merrill Prentice Hall.

Silverman, L. (1993). The gifted individual. In L. K. Silverman (Ed.), *Counseling the gifted and talented* (pp. 3–28). Denver, CO: Love.

Silverman, L. (1998) Through the lens of giftedness. *Roeper Review, 20*, 204–210.

Silverman, L. (1999) Perfectionism. *Gifted International, 13*, 216–255.

Sisk, D. (1983). *Land of the sphinx and land of the rainbow.* Tampa: University of South Florida.

Zimmerman, B. J. (2006). Enhancing students' academic responsibility and achievement. In R. J. Sternberg & R. F. Subotnik (Eds.), *Optimizing student success with other three Rs* (pp. 179–198). Greenwich, CT: Information Age.

4

Moral Courage

Ramon lives for playing basketball, and when his team wins, the excitement he feels is unsurpassed by any of his sixteen years of life experiences. The practices and long hours of planning and learning plays is no problem for him; he is willing to make any sacrifice for the team. They are like a family to him. Several members of the team are in his advanced placement math and chemistry classes, and two have gone to school with him since elementary school. Everything has been great with his team, until after the last game, when the players all wanted him to go to Joe's house to get high. Ramon declined and went home alone. When his father noted his early arrival from the game, he asked why he was home early. Ramon told his father about the team and their "pot party." His father calmly pointed out that Ramon was at a choice-point.

Ramon, like many young people, is faced with choice-points on a daily basis when the behavior of classmates and friends violate his moral principles of what is right and what is wrong. If Ramon tells the coach, the players might get kicked off the team and he would lose friends. He would be viewed as a "snitch" and the team would lose their opportunity to compete for the state championship. Yet, he knows what they are doing is wrong. He wants to have the courage to stand up for what he thinks is right.

Ramon spoke to his priest, who agreed with Ramon's father and said, "You must act on your principles, and have the courage to face the consequences." Ramon decided to tell the coach, who immediately called in the team and confronted them about the party. They looked with hatred and contempt at Ramon. The coach suspended the five young men who attended the pot party, all of whom were first-string players. Word of what happened traveled swiftly around the school, and Ramon found very few students would either talk to him or sit with him at lunch. He continued to work with the other basketball players, and a tight rapport developed among them as they tried to overcome the loss of the first-string players. Amazingly, the team won the next two games, and they were able to compete for the state championship.

In this chapter, we explore the concept of moral courage and examine the actions of Ramon, who stood up for his values, as the essence of moral courage. The three strands of moral courage proposed by Rushworth Kidder (2003) are discussed, and the core values of compassion, honesty, fairness, responsibility, and respect identified by Gorbachev and colleagues in San Francisco are explored.

Research on the use of moral dilemmas with secondary students is introduced, and an example of a moral dilemma from a study is shared. Results from the study indicate that it is possible to promote the development of moral courage in gifted students using moral dilemmas. Strategies to develop moral courage are then examined, including the study of myths and of eminent people.

STANDING UP FOR VALUES IS THE ESSENCE OF MORAL COURAGE

Having the moral courage to act on their principles is very important for gifted students, because they have a keen sense of right and wrong, as well as a sense of fairness. Silverman (1994) reported that gifted students have a passion for justice, are profoundly aware, and experience life with great intensity, and that these traits appear to correlate with moral sensitivity in childhood and ethical development in adult life.

Moral Courage Defined

Rushworth Kidder (2003) said in *Moral Courage* there are three strands that define moral courage: (1) a commitment to moral principles, (2) an awareness of the danger involved in supporting these principles, and (3) a willingness to endure danger, with its consequences. Kidder stressed that acts of moral courage have risks of humiliation, ridicule, and contempt. Ramon experienced humiliation, ridicule, and contempt, and the first-string team players called him a "snitch." Even his friends from elementary school called him a "chicken" and made fun of the "goodie-boy."

Research on Core Values

In 1996, Mikhail Gorbachev convened a meeting in San Francisco to engage 272 global thinkers in a series of interviews to identify core values. The results from this effort have been used in seminars with young people and adults in both the United States and overseas by the Institute for Global Ethics. The core values they identified included compassion, honesty, fairness, responsibility, and respect. The group concluded that these values were at the heart of humanity's search for shared values.

Dyson (2004) reported on a training session in West Vancouver in which Kidder, the founder of the Institute for Global Ethics, shared ideas about the need to build what he called *ethical fitness* to build moral arguments. Dyson said the more students and teachers understand the issues they face every time they make a decision, the better conclusions they will make.

Using Moral Dilemmas to Promote the Development of Moral Courage

Dabrowski's Theory of Emotional Development addresses a core of personal characteristics that distinguish the behavior of gifted students. Dabrowski said that it is in the nature of many gifted students to steadfastly uphold the principles they believe in and to attempt to be individuals who are true to themselves (Dabrowski, 1964). This description of moral courage is similar to what Loevinger & Wessler (1970) called *ego maturity*. They developed an Ego Maturity Scale that uses a ten-point scale that has milestones of ego development from a presocial stage, in which the infant constructs for himself or herself a stable world of objects and separates out a self as object, to an autonomous stage. They include the presocial stage in their conceptual framework, but it is not measured on the scale.

In Stage 1 on the Ego Maturity Scale, or the Impulse Stage, the child is governed by impulses that affirm the sense of self through immediate rewards and punishments. In Stage 2, the Self-Protective Stage, the child is concerned with a fear of being caught, externalizes blame, and is opportunistic. There is concern of being controlling and being controlled. In Stage 3, the Conformity Stage, there is conformity to external rules and an interest in competition. In this stage, the school age child identifies with authority, the parents, other adults, and their peers.

In Stage 4, the Conscientious Stage, the student is reflective, and self-evaluated standards, self-consciousness, and self-confidence have appeared. The individual is self-critical, but aware of choices and strives for goals. Achievement is important in this stage, and it is measured by the student's own inner standards rather than being primarily a matter of competition and social approval. In this stage, absolute standards and rules are often replaced with ones in a cooperative and contingent form. The Stage 4 person views life as presenting choices, and he or she is not a pawn of fate. This person feels in charge of his or her destiny. Stage 4 individuals have differentiated feelings and concern for communication. The Stage 4–5 (the transition from Conscientious to Autonomous) person evidences greater complexity in his or her concept of interpersonal interaction, in physiological causality, and in the concept of individuality (Loevinger & Wessler, 1970). Clearly, we would want gifted students to operate at Stage 4 and 5, and to be capable of using their potential in positive constructive endeavors to manifest moral courage. In Stage 5, the Autonomous Stage, the individual is concerned with social problems beyond his or her immediate experience, and striving for achievement is partially supplanted by self-fulfillment. This stage is similar to self-actualization as described by Maslow (1954) and Level V of Dabrowski's (1964) theory.

What Does Research Say About Moral Courage?

To address the question of whether it is possible to promote moral courage in gifted and talented students, a study was conducted using the strategies of discussion and moral dilemmas (Sisk, 2003). Twenty-three gifted students participated, and they were encouraged to engage in self-observation and self-analysis to reflect on their values and on the values of others. They were introduced to the concept that for a belief to become your own, it has to follow a process in which you freely choose it from alternatives after thoughtful consideration of consequences. The value is prized and cherished, publicly affirmed, acted upon in reality, and acted upon repeatedly. This process was adapted from the work of Raths, Harmin, and Simon (1978) in *Values and Teaching: Working With Values in the Classroom*.

The twenty-three students were participants in a three-week summer residential program for gifted students, and included eleven girls and twelve boys, all age 16. Each evening from 7 PM to 9 PM, the group read and discussed a moral dilemma, using a simple discussion format of *What, So What*, and *Now What*. *What* included summarizing the dilemma. *So What* was the opinion of the students, or what they thought about it. *Now What* was how they could apply the dilemma to their own lives and the significance of the dilemma. The students were administered a pretest and a post-test using the Loevinger-Wessler scale, and each student kept a daily journal for personal reflection. An example of a moral dilemma used in the study follows.

CASE STUDY

Sara, who is 13, has a 16-year-old brother named Dylan. They share ideas and talk about almost everything, including boyfriends and girlfriends. When school started in September, Dylan began hanging around with some new kids. He began to lose weight, and his personality began to change. He had always been a happy-go-lucky person, but now he is always fearful and nervous. Sara and Dylan's parents are very concerned and worried about him. At dinner, they ask if there is anything wrong, but Dylan says that they are just being overly concerned and that nothing is wrong.

Late one night as Sara and Dylan are talking, Dylan begins to cry, and he admits that he is taking drugs. Because the other kids that he hangs out with are doing drugs, he also has gotten involved. He shares that he has shoplifted to pay for drugs, which are very expensive.

(Continued)

(Continued)

Dylan says that the drugs make him feel very good, but that he feels sick when he can't get any. He makes Sara promise not to tell anyone what he said, especially their parents. He also promises to stop taking drugs as soon as he can.

The next day their mother asks Sara if she knows what is wrong with Dylan. She knows Sara and Dylan talk about everything and she expects Sara to tell the truth. What should Sara do?

1. Should she break Dylan's confidence?

2. Should a promise be kept?

3. Is there any way that Sara has a right to tell her mother what Dylan shared?

4. If she doesn't tell her mother, is she justified in saying she doesn't know anything?

The gifted students in the study examined the moral issues involved in ten such dilemmas, and discussed each of the dilemmas to bring the need for moral courage into a clear focus for analysis.

The pretest to post-test changes on the Loevinger-Wessler Ego Maturity Instrument using a ten-point scale indicate a significant shift from Stage 3 (Conformity) and Stage 3–4 (transition from Conformity to Conscientious) toward Stage 4 (Conscientious), Stage 4–5 (transition from Conscientious to Autonomous), and Stage 5 (Autonomous) during the ten weekly sessions. Twenty-one of the twenty-three gifted adolescent students in the original study completed the follow-up testing. The scores of the students on the Loevinger-Wessler scale are shown in Table 4.1.

Table 4.1   Loevinger-Wessler Scores Using a Ten-Point Scale

	N	Mean Score	Standard Deviation	t-value	p-value, 1-tailed	df
Pre	21	6.29	0.78	1.79	0.005	20
Post	21	6.67	1.07	4.56	0.001	20
One year follow-up	21	7.38	0.97			

This study indicated that it is possible to promote the development of moral courage in gifted students using discussion and moral dilemmas. As Conscientious to Autonomous level students, all twenty-three students opted for Sara to tell her mother. Discussions of moral dilemmas can be integrated into social studies, language arts, and science classes using moral dilemmas that are appropriate to each content area. The gifted students wrote in their journals that they enjoyed the discussions, that the dilemmas were "cool," and that they could apply what they were learning in the discussions to their daily life at school and at home. The teachers of the students who assisted in the one year follow-up assessment said, "The summer experience led to more effective student responses in the classroom when real moral dilemmas were presented."

STRATEGIES TO BUILD MORAL COURAGE

Building Moral Courage by Organizing and Using Themes in Myths

Moral courage is developed through facing the challenges of life with commitment and strength, but gifted students can accomplish this same development of moral courage vicariously and safely by reading stories and myths of Greek gods, Norse heroes, Polynesian tricksters, and Native American warriors, which are full of profound moral lessons about life. By reading and discussing myths through shared inquiry and discussion, gifted students quickly recognize that myths are related to real-life problems. Myths have a mysterious capacity to contain and communicate paradoxes, and they encourage gifted students to experience complex relationships and ideas to help them formulate their own ideas.

Myths also encourage gifted students to see through, around, and over any moral dilemmas they may be experiencing. One dilemma many gifted students face is the high expectations of their parents, and the spoken and unspoken message, "You are to carry on our family name to higher and higher levels of accomplishment." To address this dilemma, the theme of "Parents and Children" was used in enrichment classes for gifted students with the objective of exploring "truths" in myths.

Parents and Children Theme

To explore the theme of "Parents and Children," gifted students can read about Thetis and Achilles, the story of how parents expect nothing less than everything from their children. The theme of this Greek myth revolves around the ambition Thetis has for her child—she wants her son to be a god. In the myth, Thetis conveys tremendous insight into the secret hopes, longings, and dreams that parents may unknowingly and knowingly ask of their gifted children. Thetis, the goddess mother, wants her child to be divine like her rather than mortal like the father. Another myth, of Orion and Oenopion, was also used to explore the "Parents and Children" theme. In this story, a father attempts to totally possess his daughter and to make all her decisions for her.

Gifted students can keep daily journals to help them assess their level of understanding concerning the myths and the moral dilemmas. Journaling helps gifted students recognize their ability to apply the concepts to their lives. After reading the two myths, a group of gifted adolescents shared sacrifices their own parents had made for them, and how when they failed in school work, music, and swimming competitions, their parents were disappointed or angry. Such discussions can help gifted students build a better understanding of the world and how it works, but more importantly the study of myths can help gifted students build a better understanding of themselves in relation to others in using their moral courage. Other themes and myths that can be used to build moral courage include the following.

Themes and Myths

- Becoming an individual, including leaving home (*Peredur, the Son of Evrawc*)
- Fighting for autonomy (*Gilgamesh and the Tree of Life*)
- Pursuing the quest for meaning (*Perseus*)
- Position and power, including finding a vocation (*A Myth of Two Brothers*)
- Greed and ambition (*King Midas*)
- Responsibility (*King Minos and the Bull*)
- Rites of passage, separation loss, and suffering (*Orpheus and Eurydice*)
- Spiritual quest (*Parsifal*)

Gifted students, with their well-developed reasoning and ability to engage in higher levels of thinking, of analyzing and synthesizing information, can step back from the reading of the myth and make applications to themselves and the development of their moral courage. One student shared the following in her journal:

> I like the fact that instead of just reading the myths, we can discuss them, and we can have our own feelings. When I read about Thetis and Achilles, I saw my mom in Thetis. She drags me to every audition for modeling, and she "eyes" every bite of anything I eat until I want to scream. She wants so much for me. She entered me into one contest and told them I was a teenager when I was 11. I just stood there and let her tell that lie—now I would use my moral courage and refuse to go. (Aeisha, age 15)

Aeisha was involved in a project for eighty-five gifted middle school students in Texas called Mythic Journey. This project provided the students ten weekly sessions from 9 AM to 11 AM on Saturday at a local university to explore and to develop their moral courage. This type of study of myths can be integrated into a language arts or social studies class to explore multicultural leadership.

Using the Study of Eminent People to Build Moral Courage

Studying eminent people can help gifted students recognize the moral courage demonstrated by others, and develop an understanding of the importance of developing moral courage. A case study with Mr. Peck and his middle school language arts class demonstrates how this strategy can be used with gifted students.

CASE STUDY

Mr. Peck, a middle school language arts teacher greeted his seventh grade students as they entered the room. Jarrod eagerly asked, "Can I go first in talking about our study of eminent people with moral courage?" Mr. Peck smiled and said, "Why not, you can set the stage for our discussion. You investigated Gandhi, didn't you?"

"Yes," said Jarrod. "Gandhi was showing moral courage even as a young man in South Africa, when they forced him to ride in the 'colored car.'" Mr. Peck smiled and said, "Your study of Gandhi is really causing you to think about his relevance as a model." He then urged the students to quickly take their seats. Mr. Peck asked them to take out their journals, to jot down responses to the individual reports on eminent people, and to look for similarities in their lives and in their responses.

Prior to selecting an eminent person as a research topic, the students had discussed moral courage and agreed to use the three strand description of Rushworth Kidder (2003) to identify people with moral courage: (1) a commitment to moral principles; (2) an awareness of the danger involved in supporting these principles; and (3) a willingness to endure that danger, with its consequences.

Mr. Peck called on Jarrod, "Are you ready with your report on Gandhi?" Jarrod nodded and approached the front of the class to begin his PowerPoint presentation. He shared that Gandhi was born in 1869 near Bombay, and he was an average student in school. "Like some of us" Jarrod interjected. Then he said, "Gandhi went on to study law in London." Smiling, Jarrod added, "Perseverance was one of his characteristics." He stressed that Gandhi read the *Bhagavad Gita*, a Hindu epic poem that became his calling, to undertake a battle of righteousness. "The *Gita* as it was known," said Jarrod, "influenced Gandhi to devote himself to the service of his fellow man, and he was influenced by Ahimsa, the ancient Hindu ideal of nonviolence to all living things."

At this point, Paul raised his hand and said, "Martin Luther King, my eminent person, was influenced by Gandhi." Susan added, "Mandela traveled to India to meet Gandhi, and he followed his ideas of nonviolence." Mr. Peck smiled and said, "These are great observations. Be sure and list them in your journal so we can discuss the interconnections of these eminent people and their demonstration of moral courage."

Jarrod continued, "Gandhi and a number of followers marched 240 miles in 24 days to make their own salt from the sea, as an act of defiance of British colonial laws that denied the Indian people from making their own salt. By the time they reached the sea, several thousand people had joined in the march, and all along the coast other marches were being carried out by other people who knew of Gandhi's march. All totaled, during their marches, more than 60,000 people were arrested, including Gandhi."

Jarrod paused, obviously caught up in the drama of his report, and several students added that their eminent people had been imprisoned because of their commitment to nonviolence principles, including Ralph Waldo Emerson, Martin Luther King, Jr., and Nelson Mandela.

Jarrod summarized his report by saying, "Gandhi was convinced that mass noncooperation could achieve independence for India. And he said, 'You cannot be dominated unless you cooperate with your dominators.'" Jarrod concluded by emphasizing, "Gandhi taught that we should value civil liberties and the individual rights of all human beings, and he lived for and was killed for preaching tolerance."

(Continued)

(Continued)

Paul solemnly added, "So was Martin Luther King, Jr. He died for the same principles." Melanie added, "My person, Helen Keller believed in nonviolence. She spoke out against American preparedness in World II, and she was really criticized. She identified with Joan of Arc, and said she would not change her ideas about helping poor people and nonviolence, even if she were placed in jail."

Mr. Peck asked the class to acknowledge Jarrod's presentation, which they did with enthusiastic clicking, which they had previously decided to use instead of clapping for one another. Jarrod smiled and said, "I just wish all my school work could be this interesting." Mr. Peck chuckled. He asked the class to write in their journals and to use the last fifteen minutes of class for discussion. He then walked around acknowledging the comments of connection made by Paul, Susan, and Melanie.

Susan said, "Can I read something, even if it isn't my turn to present?" Mr. Peck recognized her enthusiasm and eagerness to share, and he said, "Sure." Susan read from Martin Luther King, Jr.'s, acceptance speech for his Nobel Prize:

I conclude that this award is a profound recognition that nonviolence is the answer to the crucial political and moral questions of our time, the need for man to overcome oppression and violence.

Mr. Peck thought for a moment, and then said, "Tomorrow when Susan gives her presentation, she will be using direct speeches of Martin Luther King, Jr., in his own words, so we will be able to hear his passionate commitment."

The class began noting ideas in their journals, and then joined in a lively discussion in which they identified similarities between their eminent people, including Winston Churchill, Albert Einstein, Ralph Waldo Emerson, Thomas Jefferson, Abraham Lincoln, Helen Keller, Eleanor Roosevelt, Mother Teresa, and Nikola Tesla.

In a conversation with his fellow teachers, Mr. Peck said, "That class was like consciousness exploring itself. Those kids amaze me when their minds take off." Providing opportunities for gifted kids to explore how moral courage affects the lives of individuals, and how their actions affect society, can truly help great kids be greater.

HELP FOR STUDENTS TO EXPLORE MORAL COURAGE IN DILEMMAS

Nielsen (2006) suggested a number of questions based on the work of Kidder (2003) that teachers can use to help gifted students explore moral courage in dilemmas. Three questions that focus on key values or principles, internal fears or risks, and personal trusts are as follows.

What Key Values or Principles Seemed Most at Stake?

- Honesty (truthfulness, integrity)
- Fairness (justice)

- Respectfulness (tolerance and respect for self, family, elders, others, and life itself)
- Responsibility (self-discipline)
- Compassion (empathy, mercy, love, generosity)

What Internal Fears or Risks Contributed to the Dilemma?

- Fear of ambiguity
- Fear of public exposure
- Fear of personal loss

What Personal Trusts Allowed the Person to Be Willing to Endure the Risks?

- Trust based on previous experience
- Trust in his/her own moral and ethical character
- Trust based on intuition or gut reaction
- Trust based on faith
- Trust based on supportive context (even a community of one)

Kidder (2003) asked why moral courage matters so much to us in these days, and then answered his question with numerous examples of the lack of moral courage in corporate settings, legal proceedings, politics, sports, and entertainment. He suggested that what is needed today is a way to encourage and to develop moral courage in our students. Schools are an excellent place for students to have opportunities to explore and express moral courage, such as the students in Mr. Peck's class and their study of eminent people.

Standing up for values is the major feature of moral courage, but having values, and living by values are very different. As students discuss moral courage, exploring it in myths and in the lives of eminent people, they can relate moral courage to their individual daily lives. The challenge for schools is to commit to the development of moral courage and to provide a climate that allows moral courage to be implemented and to be nurtured in the classroom.

SUMMARY

In this chapter, we explored the concept of moral courage and examined the actions of Ramon, who stood up for his values, as the essence of moral courage. Moral courage was defined by Rushworth Kidder (2003) as having three strands: (1) a commitment to moral principles, (2) an awareness of the danger involved in supporting these principles, and (3) a willingness to endure danger in adhering to these principles. Research on core values was examined, including the San Francisco meeting convened by

Gorbachev in which the core values of compassion, honesty, fairness, responsibility, and respect were identified.

The development of moral courage was examined and how the use of moral dilemmas can assist gifted students in exploring and developing their moral courage. The relationship between Dabrowksi's Levels IV and V and the work of Loevinger and Wessler was discussed, with similarities in stressing the importance of autonomy and using positive constructive endeavors to manifest moral courage.

Research on the use of moral dilemmas with secondary gifted students was explored, and an example of a moral dilemma from the study was examined. Results from the study indicate that it is possible to promote the development of moral courage in gifted students using discussion of moral dilemmas. The use of the study of myths, organized around themes, was introduced as another strategy to build moral courage, as well as the study of eminent people. A case study in a language arts class was examined to note how the study of eminent people can enable gifted students to explore moral courage in action.

The next chapter focuses on individuality and how students can go about becoming more aware of their gifts and of ways to develop them. The task of taking responsibility for one's actions and commitment to personal and individual excellence is explored.

Teacher Voice

Not a day passes here in middle school without seeing at least one child fight with the idea of doing what is right and just. I hear my students voice their fears of being called a "snitch" or being beat up for telling the truth or warning the teachers or administration of a situation. So many of them have learned these values from within not only their peer groups, but also their families. Fortunately, there are always those whose moral courage wins the battle and, yes, these are usually, but not always, my gifted students. I would like to see more encouragement of moral courage through open discussion in school. With moral courage comes the ability to think and reason, a skill that enables gifted students to succeed in life as well as academics. I will make it a requirement for myself to support and encourage them to consider the "choice moments" in their daily lives. When I think of moral courage, I can't help but think of the Cowardly Lion from *The Wizard of Oz*. Like him, I know the gifted student's moral courage has been inside them all along; they just have to be willing to accept it.

Stacey Castolenia
Teacher, grades 6–8

Read On

Ayers, R., & Crawford, A. (Eds.). (2004). *Great books for high school kids: A teacher's guide to books that can change teens lives.* Boston: Beacon Press.

Johnson, D. (2003). *Reaching out: Interpersonal effectiveness and self-actualization.* New York: Allyn & Bacon.

Kaye, S., & Thomson, P. (2007). *Philosophy for teens: Questioning life's big ideas.* Austin, TX: Prufrock Press.

Kidder, R. (1994). *Shared values for a troubled world: Conversations with men and women of conscience.* San Francisco: Jossey Press.

Sisk, D. (2001). The mythic journey. *Understanding Our Gifted, 13*(3), 18–19.

Log On

Decisions! Decisions! (http://www.lifestreamcenter.net/DrB/Lessons/decisions/). In this Web quest, students can explore their values and consider the decisions they make at various stages of their life.

Everyday Heroes (http://schoolweb.missouri.edu/poplarbluff.k12.mo.us/lowe/webquest .html). This Web quest invites students to become members of their local television station, with the task of producing a television show called "Everyday Heroes."

The Hero's Journey. (http://www.mcli.dist.maricopa.edu/smc/journey). This Web site assists students in exploring classical myths, as well as how to create their own life stories.

Monomyth (http://ias.berkeley.edu/orias/hero/index.htm). This Berkeley Education Web site provides a digital library of materials for teachers in mythology, using the theme of the hero's journey.

Reflect On

- Rushworth Kidder (2003) talks about the capacity and willingness to endure risk in using moral courage in situations. Think of a situation in which you or someone you know used moral courage. Did you trust in your past experiences, in your faith, in a gut feeling, or in your personal character?
- Robert Kennedy said that moral courage is a rarer commodity than bravery in battle or great intelligence; yet it is the one essential vital quality for those who seek to change a world that yields most painfully to change. What thoughts come to mind from this quotation?
- Mass killings and genocides have occurred in numerous places in the past century. Each time, humanity says never again. Yet, it does continue to occur. What is in our consciousness that allows us to treat other human beings so inhumanely?

REFERENCES

Ayers, R., & Crawford, A. (Eds.). (2004). *Great books for high school kids: A teacher's guide to books that can change teens lives.* Boston: Beacon Press.

Dabrowski, K. (1964). *Positive disintegration.* Boston: Little, Brown.

Dyson, L. (2004). Right versus right. *Adminvo,* Vancouver, BC, 16–17.

Johnson, D. (2003). *Reaching out: Interpersonal effectiveness and self-actualization.* New York: Allyn & Bacon.

Kaye, S., & Thomson, P. (2007). *Philosophy for teens: Questioning life's big ideas.* Austin, TX: Prufrock Press.

Kidder, R. (1994). *Shared values for a troubled world: Conversations with men and women of conscience.* San Francisco: Jossey Press.

Kidder, R. (2003). *Moral courage.* New York: HarperCollins.

Loevinger, J., & Wessler, R. (1970). *The measuring of ego development.* San Francisco: Jossey Press.

Maslow, A. (1954). *Motivation and personality.* New York: Harper & Row.

Nielsen, E. (2006, November). *Exploring moral courage through music, film, and books*. A presentation at the National Association for Gifted Children, Charlotte, NC.

Raths, L., Harmin, K., & Simon, S. (1978). *Values and teaching: Working with values in the classroom*. Columbus, OH: Charles E. Merrill.

Silverman, L (1994). The moral sensitivity of gifted children and the evolution of society. *Roeper Review, 17,* 110–116.

Sisk, D. (2001). The mythic journey. *Understanding Our Gifted, 13*(3), 18–19.

Sisk, D. (2003). Gifted with behavior disorders: Marching to different drummers. In D. Montgomery (Ed.), *Gifted & talented children with special needs* (pp. 131–154). London: David Fulton.

5

Individuality

Knowing Oneself

Jeremy has not been identified for his middle school gifted program. However, his sister Lisa, two years older was identified in elementary school. She is on the high school debate team, has won accolades in University Interscholastic League (UIL) competitions, and her accomplishments are "highlighted" by teachers with comments such as, "Aren't you Lisa's brother?" "You know she is one of our star students." In response to these comments, Jeremy usually shrugs. If he were asked, he would probably say, "I know, I know." Even his parents don't view him as gifted, but in his math and science classes, when he is interested, he often amazes his teachers with his questions and advanced content knowledge.

In the following conversation, Lisa and Jeremy talk about their beliefs, about their capabilities to succeed, their expectations for future success, and their interest and value for school work.

"How did you do on that social studies test you were studying for last night? Was it hard or easy?" Lisa asked. Jeremy sighed and replied, "It was boring, who wants to know all that stuff from the past—what does it have to do with my life?" Lisa chuckled and said, "What happened before does matter today. You can see how, in many ways, we keep on making the same mistakes." She paused and continued, "I like social studies, I might even major in sociology in college." Jeremy groaned and replied, "Get real; I hate those true and false questions. And when you have to write papers, I never know what to say. I would rather do labs in science—you know cutting up frogs and stuff. But we never do labs." He added, "We do science out of books, and how stupid is that?" Lisa nodded and said, "I know. We do that in some of my classes in high school too. But Jeremy, you should try to be in UIL. You can win scholarships for college by being good in drama." Jeremy laughed and replied, "Drama? Are you kidding, Lisa? I clam up." He made a clam shutting gesture with his hand and they both laughed.

Lisa leaned toward to her brother and said, "You are so goofy, little brother, but you are a whiz in math—remember how you had to help me with my geometry?" Jeremy shrugged and replied, "I'm barely getting a C in my math class. Having to show your work when you already "just know" the answer is stupid. I'm really not good at anything that has to do with school." Then he added enthusiastically, "Music is what I am able to do. The only thing I really enjoy is banging away on my drums after school, and making up my own songs." Lisa sighed and said, "But remember, school prepares you for college, and college prepares you for life." Jeremy shrugged again, and said, "Swell, I think I'll get a C in life too."

In this chapter, we examine the role of expectancies, discuss self-perception of ability, and show how they both affect the efforts of gifted students to know themselves and to achieve individuality. A model of self-awareness is introduced, and examples of activities to build self-understanding, including the *I* and *You* buttons, are discussed. The importance of gifted students taking responsibility for their actions is addressed, and activities to help gifted kids prioritize their roles and tasks is introduced.

Jeremy is a great example of a gifted student whose self-perception of ability is one of never being able to live up to the standards and expectations people have for his sister, Lisa. In many ways, Jeremy is unaware of his gifts, and he doesn't have a clue on ways to develop them. Lisa and Jeremy share comments about whether they like a subject, whether it is important to them, or relevant. Their values and beliefs are key factors in their discussion, as well as in their expectations. Expectancies and values are important for predicting the future choice behavior of gifted students, their engagement, persistence, and actual achievement. Gifted students may have confidence they can do well and expect to succeed, but if they don't value the task or assignment, they are less likely to choose to become engaged. On the other hand, gifted students may think a task or activity is interesting or important, but if they think they can't do it, they may not even attempt the activity or lesson.

CHANGING STUDENTS' BELIEFS ABOUT LEARNING

One major way to change students' beliefs about learning is to foster the belief that competence or ability is a changeable, controllable aspect of development. Some students take longer to master some skills than others, and it is helpful when teachers and parents communicate positive high expectations for their students and children. This type of communication is demonstrated by Mr. Eason talking with Jeremy and the other students in his social studies class.

CASE STUDY

Mr. Eason says, "Class, I want to talk with you about how you went about studying for the social studies test." Several students raise their hands and one says, "I reread the chapter, especially the parts I had underlined, for an hour or two." Another adds, "I concentrated on my notes, and reread them the night before and the morning of the test." One student says "I studied with Paul, and we asked one another questions in the evening before, and we used his treadmill while answering the questions. Sometimes, we drew pictures to help us remember the material." Still another student adds, "I outlined the chapter and made study cards, and it took all evening." Mr. Eason says, "All of you are using different strategies to study, different levels of effort and amounts of time. I would like to emphasize that effort, the amount of time spent studying, and the use of different learning strategies can help all of you to do better."

He then lists the study skills they identified for future consideration:

- Rereading
- Note taking
- Making pictures
- Outlining
- Use a study buddy to formulate questions

"The last point I want to make in this discussion," says Mr. Eason, "is that I have high expectations for all of you, and all of you can do well in this class." He goes on to say, "I know that many of you have trouble seeing the relevance of social studies in your lives, so I have developed a 3×5 card for you to fill out after each class with a study buddy, to identify the major ideas for each class." Mr. Eason's card is depicted in Figure 5.1.

Figure 5.1   Social Studies Class Summary Card

Today's topic:
_____

One key idea

was _____

This idea is important

because _____

Another key idea

was _____

This idea is important

because _____

These ideas are useful

when _____

(Continued)

The discussion with Mr. Eason and his class reinforced and built on the existing study strategies of his students, and the use of the summary card will serve as a great summarizing tool and will help the students and the teacher bring closure to each lesson.

What Does Research Say About Expectations and Perceptions of Ability?

In a series of large-scale correlational field studies, Eccles and Wigfield (1993, 1995) and their colleagues investigated the role of expectations and ability perceptions in achievement. Upper elementary and middle school students were given self-report measures of their self-perception of ability and expectancy for success, as well as task value beliefs in mathematics and language arts at the beginning of a school year and at the end of the same year. These studies consistently found that students' self-perception of ability and their expectations for success were the strongest predictors of grades in mathematics and language arts.

The research on expectancy and value beliefs suggest a number of implications for teachers and parents. One major implication is the need to help students maintain relatively accurate, but high expectations and perceptions of their competency. Another implication is the need to help students develop accurate and positive self-concepts. The research on students' perception of their competence and self-concept is similar. Shunk, Pintrich, and Meece (2008) report that helping students develop positive values about school learning is important in building interest in learning and is equally important in helping students develop positive and accurate views of their talents.

Help for Developing Awareness of One's Talents

The consciousness of self is not just an intellectual idea. The argument of Descarte for the existence of self—"I think, therefore I am"—is not enough. As psychologist Rollo May (1953) stated:

> We experience ourselves as a thinking-intuiting-feeling, and acting unit. The self is then not merely the sum of the various roles one plays—it is the capacity by which one knows one plays these roles; it is the center from which one sees and is aware of these so-called different "sides" of self. (p. 72)

May's concept of the individual as a thinking/intuiting/feeling/acting unit can be expressed in an awareness of self model depicted in Figure 5.2, adapted from Shallcross and Sisk (1982, p. 16).

Figure 5.2   Awareness of Self Model

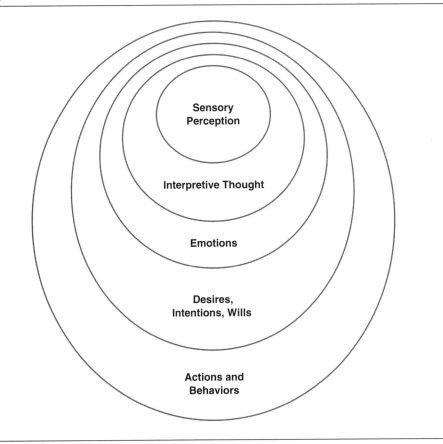

Getting in Touch With Our Senses

An activity that can be used with gifted students to help them get in touch with their senses is the use of unfinished sensory thoughts. Students can choose a topic such as "Walk in the Woods" and use the following phrases as a starting point.

I see_____

I hear_____

I touch_____

I feel_____

I taste_____

I experience_____

A completed sensory thought activity of a gifted sixth grade student, demonstrates the use of the framework.

Walk in the Woods

I see *the tall trees.*

I hear *the rustling leaves.*

I touch *the smooth moss on the trees.*

I feel *calm and quiet.*

I see *the rain coming down through the limbs.*

I taste *the drops as they fall on my tongue.*

I hear *the drops fall on the leaves.*

I experience *being part of nature.*

Interpretive Thoughts

After writing her thoughts, Roz said, "I really felt like I took a walk in the woods, especially tasting the drops of rain on my tongue." Our senses provide us the raw data; what we do with that data is the interpretive part of awareness. Roz went on to say, "We really need to take care of our forests, and make sure they are there for us, to get away from the city, and for the animals as well."

Emotions

Feelings and emotions are within us, and as students feel or experience them, they then spontaneously respond. Dabrowski's Theory of Emotional Development says our emotions or "intensities" are there to help us develop our talents, particularly, our creative talents. In today's world, many people have learned to hide their feelings, and we use phrases like "having it altogether" that connote a "cool" presentation to others. However, the price paid for hiding feelings is the possibility that others may never know who we really are (Silverman, 1998).

Exploring Emotions Through Sociodrama

In sociodrama, a social problem is identified and the student actors are selected. Then the students can be instructed to spontaneously act out the drama, as well as to turn aside and share their feelings and emotions in a different voice from the one they use in the sociodrama. Shakespeare used this "soliloquy technique," when his actors stepped forward from the rest of the cast and voiced their feelings about what was being revealed in the scene.

A fourth grade group of gifted students, studying early explorations as a theme, role-played an interaction between the Native Americans and the colonial settlers in the northeast United States. The students researched the bartering between the settlers and the Native Americans. Their dialogue follows:

Eric, role-playing a settler, said, "Here are some fine things that you will enjoy—a mirror, and look how you can see yourself." He gestured with the mirror and then said, "Also, these are lovely beads for you. See how the sun catches the light." Ralph, role-playing a Native American, looked with amazement at the mirror and beads, and smiled widely. Then Eric stepped forward away from the Native American and in an aside, or soliloquy, said, "How foolish he is. The mirror and beads are worthless, and he is willing to trade them for beaver skins—a fool is born every day."

When Miss Browne, the teacher, discussed the sociodrama with the students, she asked Eric, "What made you say a fool is born every day?" Eric replied, "My grandfather says that when he thinks someone is being taken advantage of, like in all the commercials for different products on television." At which point Eric added, "I think most times, asides are what we think and don't necessarily say." Miss Browne nodded in affirmation of his analytical thinking, and said, "But, how could a playwright show what someone is thinking, if they don't use an aside?" Emily responded, "On television there is a voice that you can hear, and that is what the person is thinking." The teacher added, "Great observation, Emily. I'm glad we had this time to explore sociodrama, and how our feelings can be hidden in situations." Melanie said, "It's like when someone says, how do you like something they are serving for dinner, and you say it's OK, but an aside would be: it's awful."

In this brief activity, these fourth grade gifted students explored how sociodrama can help clarify social themes, and they discussed the important function emotions have in building self-awareness.

Desires, Intentions, and Wills

Desires represent what one wants to accomplish or to have. Intentions can be both desires or wills, and they can be short term or long term. Another way to look at intentions or desires is to think of them as objectives. One objective might be to offer to do something nice for someone, and this objective could become an intention. Intentions can be hidden when we feel they are in conflict with other intentions. For example, "I want to write a great novel," may be in conflict with "I want to have more time for fun and not to work hard."

One conflict that gifted teenage students often experience is wanting to do well in school while also wanting to be popular and to have fun, or wanting to get good grades but also wanting to play sports. The important aspect concerning intentions is for students to be aware of their existence, and to be particularly aware of conflicts between their intentions.

Actions and Behaviors

The last component of the model of self-awareness is action or behavior. Actions are the part of us that are most often noticed and reported by others. One way for students to view their action is through the use of videotapes and digital video. Video allows students to see their facial expressions and posture, and to hear voice characteristics and inflections. They can see themselves in action with one another, as well as notice how well they listen, build on one another's ideas, express emotions, and socially interact. After one videotape session Anthony said, "I had no idea how expressive my face was. When I don't like something someone says, it is all over my face. Also, I noticed when we are really listening, we lean forward."

The self-awareness model can be used to help gifted students become more aware of themselves by consciously examining the component parts of self—sensing, interpreting, emoting, desiring, intending, willing, and behaving.

KNOWING ONESELF INVOLVES SELF-UNDERSTANDING

Effective leadership in our global world calls for people to have self-understanding, self-acceptance, and self-expression. Gifted kids can benefit from reflecting on questions such as: How do I see myself? Am I aware of my behavior and its effect on others? Do I accept myself? What is self anyway?

A sense of self evolves from our accumulated experiences and the messages received from others. Self-concept is the belief that we hold about our being, and we act according to how we feel about our self. As the research on expectations has shown, we form a concept of ourselves, what we are capable of, and what we can or cannot do, on the basis of how we experience our self.

Activities to Build Self-Understanding

Think of yourself as a musical instrument. Select one instrument and list as many adjectives as you can to describe the instrument. Now, in front of each adjective, insert the words *I am*.

In response to this activity, one ninth grade gifted student selected a piano. He described the piano as lively, versatile, responsive, and clear-cut. When he added *I am*, he said, "I am lively, I am versatile, I am responsive, and I am clear-cut." Then in a moment of insight, he said, "Holy smoke, that is me. I try to be versatile; I have lots of interests. I also am responsive; if you need me, I'm there. And I am clear-cut. I don't beat around the bush, and I like people who say what they mean—clear-cut."

This exercise or activity is based on the notion that you project yourself onto the instrument, and it is amazingly accurate. A drum is usually lively and is identified by a fun-loving person. A mellower, laid-back individual may choose a cello.

Another activity for building self-understanding is one that a colleague, Bob Partridge, a psychiatrist, uses. He asks individuals to draw a clock with hands on the face to depict where they are in life. This is a very revealing exercise in that people make very different responses.

Maria, an eighth grade student who recently moved to the United States from Mexico, put the hands on her clock at noon, and said, "For me it is a new beginning." Tom, a tenth grade student put the hands on his clock at 10 PM, saying," I am almost finished with high school, and if anyone asked me to do this exercise as a senior, I would put it at 1 PM because my college life is just beginning." Martha, a sixth grade student put her hands on the clock at 1 PM because her parents had just divorced and she and her mother are starting over in a new home in a new city.

Pondering their response and the responses of others to open-ended activities provides opportunities for gifted students to assess where they are, and they will continue to define themselves daily as they talk, interact, create, and produce.

Become Aware of One's Gifts and Talents

An activity that has proved very effective with gifted students in helping them become more aware of their gifts and talents is the *I* and *You* button. Students are asked to draw a circle, and in the middle of the circle to place the word *I* if they are doing the activity as an individual, or *You* if they are completing a button for another student. Around the *I* they draw spokes, and on these spokes they list their individual talents, interests, strengths, and/or weaknesses. Figure 5.3 is an example of a button completed by Jeremy, whom we met in the beginning of this chapter.

Figure 5.3   An *I* Button

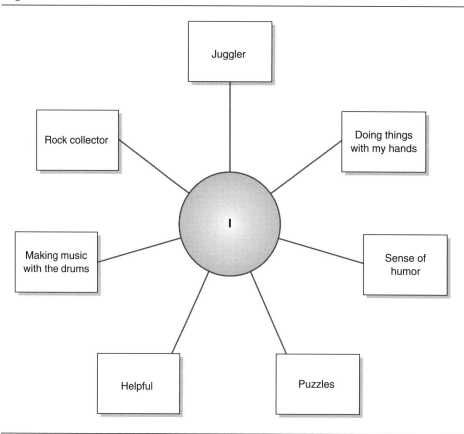

Looking at Jeremy's button, one can readily see that he is a rock collector, likes puzzles, and has a self-image of being helpful and having a sense of humor. Also, he likes making music with his drums and doing things with his hands.

This activity is nonthreatening because what students divulge with their *I* buttons is what they choose to tell and to share. After the buttons have been completed, the teacher or parent guiding the activity can ask for personal reflections on the skills and interests that have been listed.

One way to extend this activity is to have the students mill around the room, finding others with similar interests, and discover new things about one another. As they read one another's interests on the buttons, new interests may become intriguing to them, and connections can be made between others with similar interests. Still another way to use the button activity is to compare the individual perceptions of self with the perceptions of others. Lisa filled out a *You* button for her brother like the one in Figure 5.4.

Figure 5.4   A *You* Button

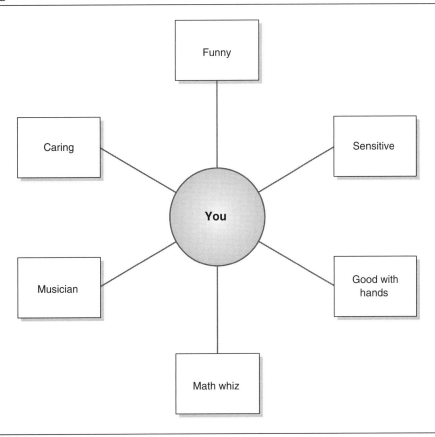

Lisa sees her brother as sensitive, caring, and funny, and she says he is good with his hands. She thinks of him as a math whiz and recognizes his talent in music. When she shared the button with him, you could see him thinking of his talents. Later on that year, he took the SAT test, and his math score of 700 surprised everyone. He participated in a Talent Identification Program and received a tuition-free course at a nearby university. His concept of himself as having a talent in math was a revelation to both him and his family. Jeremy is currently attending a school for the arts, and he has found his musical talent as well.

In his new school, Jeremy has friends who are interested in music, and he has discovered the connection between his interest in music and mathematics. He reports:

> In my old school I was intensely aware that the things I valued weren't shared by anyone. Here, I have learned that life is a journey. A journey that I must accept that has pain and confusion, but they are temporary. I know if I follow my heart, it will lead me to where I belong.

Taking Responsibility for One's Actions

Taking responsibility for one's actions involves becoming more self-directed. The first step in taking charge of your life can be initiated through examining the tasks or activities in your life. An activity that can be both revealing and fun involves making responses to a fanciful question: If you had a robot, what five things would this robot do for you?

1. _____
2. _____
3. _____
4. _____
5. _____

After answering that question, you can answer the following question: If you had a robot, what five things would the robot definitely not do for you?

1. _____
2. _____
3. _____
4. _____
5. _____

The following are selected responses from gifted kids ages 11–15 for the first question: What things would the robot do for you?

Make up my bed and clean my room. Take state tests. Do the dishes.

Hang up my clothes. Take out the garbage. Take spelling tests.

Clean the garage. Get my haircut.

Clean the litter box. Mow the backyard.

Do my homework, especially the math. Wash the car. Write essays.

In response to the second question, "What would the robot definitely not do for you?" gifted kids ages 11–15 gave the following responses.

Play basketball. Go swimming. Go fishing with my dad.

Be on the debate team. Go on family picnics. Go sailing.

Eat chocolate cake. Get As in math. Play chess.

Play video games. Hold my new kittens. Read to my baby sister.

It is obvious that most of the kids did not want the robot to do anything they liked to do. Generated lists such as these can help gifted kids reflect on what tasks have meaning for them, and then they can begin to examine their roles.

ROLES VIEWED AS TASKS

Sometimes gifted students are so involved in a large number of activities or tasks that they become frustrated because they feel inadequate as each role gets less and less of their time. The following activity can help gifted students examine their roles. It can be conducted by teachers, counselors, and parents who need to be able to listen in a nonjudgmental manner.

Role Discard Activity

List all of the roles you play in your daily life. If you have difficulty in deciding which roles to list, think of the various tasks that you complete each day. After you have listed the roles, prioritize them; the more important roles will be number one, and so on. Arthur, a 16-year-old student compiled the following list:

Friend	Brother	Altar boy
Swim team captain	Boyfriend	Student
Bag boy at grocery	Son	Grandson
Booster Club secretary	Student Council	Debate team captain
Basketball team member	Scout leader assistant	

Needless to say, Arthur is quite busy, and at the time he completed his list, he was frustrated by his lack of free time. He said, "My tasks are overwhelming." The next step in the activity is to ask the students to write each of the roles or tasks on small 2×5 cards and arrange them in the order of their importance. It helps to put the cards down on a flat area or small table so that the students can think about each role. This activity takes about ten minutes for them to think about the roles. Ask them to take the last card, discard that role, and think how it feels to discard that role.

Arthur chose to discard swim team captain, then he discarded scout leader assistant. He thought about discarding debate team captain, but decided that role was meaningful to him, and was one that he did not want to discard. Each time Arthur looked at his cards and discarded a role, he was urged by his counselor to take a quiet moment to intuitively test how he was feeling. She asked, "Are you feeling relieved, as you did with the first two discarded roles?" He said, "I'm OK with this." If he had twinges of doubt or guilt, the counselor would encourage him to examine his decision further. She reminded him, "One should not discard roles without serious consideration."

Exercises such as this one provide gifted students an opportunity to see the many and varied roles that they have assumed. The young high school student, Arthur, was somewhat surprised to find that he listed *Friend* as #1, *Son* as #2, *Grandson* as #3, *Boyfriend* as #4, and *Brother* as #5. His response to his priorities follows.

> I have always been close to my family; my father is my best friend. But since I've come to Elliott High, being a friend to others is very important to me. My girlfriend and I are not too serious, and recently my brother and I have had some problems.

In the next chapter, we examine ways for gifted students to use problem solving and creative processes to identify goals and pursue them successfully. Gifted students can learn to take charge of their lives with the help of teachers, counselors, and parents who can lend support and help them identify ways to develop their inner energies to make decisions.

SUMMARY

In this chapter, we examined the role of expectancies and self-perceptions of ability, as well as how they affect the effort of gifted students to know themselves and achieve individuality. Jeremy was an example of a student who had not been identified as gifted, and who eventually was recognized as gifted and enrolled in a special school for the arts. A case study of a social studies teacher was explored to illustrate the importance of teachers holding high expectations for students. Research was noted that found students' self-perceptions of ability and their expectations for success are the strongest predictors of grades in mathematics and language arts.

A model of self-awareness based on Rollo May's (1953) theory was introduced, with components of sensory perception, interpretive thoughts, emotions, desires, intentions, wills, and behavior. Activities for getting in touch with one's senses, exploring emotions through sociodrama, and the use of videotapes to examine one's ideas, expressions of emotion, and interaction with others were examined.

The importance of knowing oneself was stressed, and activities to build self-understanding were discussed, as well as activities to help students become aware of their gifts and talents, such as the *I* and *You* buttons.

The last set of activities suggested for use with gifted students stressed the importance of encouraging them to take responsibility for their actions, and to prioritize their many activities that can be overwhelming. This chapter addressed the importance of helping gifted students learn that they have the potential to shape themselves, and also ways to enable them to do well in school.

Teacher Voice

I see the importance of gifted students having reasonable expectations in my class. Some gifted kids have a very low perception of their ability and need to be "reinforced" a lot to do their best. I like the Self-Awareness Model because it takes you through the whole process of receiving information, examining it through your own past experiences and values, and if you get excited about it you may make goals or intentions and then action. I use something similar to that with my project-based lessons. It is essential that gifted kids take responsibility for their actions and the activities like Role Discard will be very helpful. I love the Read On, Log On, and Reflect On—they give me directions to extend the chapter. As a first year teacher, I thought the ideas were very "user friendly."

Adrienne Miranda
Middle school teacher

Read On

Burmark, L. (2002). *Visual literacy: Learn to see, see to learn.* Alexandria, VA: Association for Supervision and Curriculum Development (ASCD).

Eisner, E. (2004). Preparing for today and tomorrow. *Educational Leadership, 61*(4), 6–10.

Johnson, D. (2003). *Reaching out: Interpersonal effectiveness and self-actualization.* Boston: Allyn & Bacon (the section on self-awareness is on pp. 52–60).

Seward, K. (2004). Back to the future: The personalized education process. *Understanding Our Gifted, 16*(3), 12–13.

Log On

Education Program for Gifted Youth (EPGY) (http://www.epgy.stanford.edu/). Offers multimedia computer-based distance learning courses, optimized in pace and content.

Responsive Education Web site (http://www.responsiveeducation.org/). Examples, guidelines, and materials that schools can use to build relationships.

Virtual School for the Gifted (VSG) (http://www.vsg.edu.au/). Provides enrichment courses to extend the regular school.

Reflect On

- Do students have to value everything they learn?
- Are gifted students overly involved in activities? What effect does excessive involvement have on their expectations?

- Two theories on self have evolved in psychology: self as object and self as process. Self as object refers to the self-image as a mirror image. Self as process refers to the unique factors within the individual as determiners of self. What do you think? Could it be both?

REFERENCES

Burmark, L. (2002). *Visual literacy: Learn to see, see to learn.* Alexandria, VA: Association for Supervision and Curriculum Development (ASCD).

Eccles, J., & Wigfield, A. (1993). Negative effects of traditional middle schools on students' motivation. *Elementary School Journal, 93,* 533–574.

Eccles, J., & Wigfield, A. (1995). In the mind of the actor. The structure of adolescent achievement task values and expectancy-related beliefs. *Personality and Social Psychology Bulletin, 21,* 215–225.

Eisner, E. (2004). Preparing for today and tomorrow. *Educational Leadership, 61*(4), 6–10.

Johnson, D. (2003). *Reaching out: Interpersonal effectiveness and self-actualization.* Boston: Allyn & Bacon.

May, R. (1953). *Man's search for himself.* New York: Delta, W.W. Norton.

Seward, K. (2004). Back to the future: The personalized education process. *Understanding Our Gifted, 16*(3), 12–13.

Shallcross, D., & Sisk, D. (1982). *The growing person.* Englewood Cliffs, NJ: Prentice Hall.

Shunk, D., Pintrich, P., & Meece, J. (2008). *Motivation in education.* Columbus, OH: Merrill Prentice Hall.

Silverman, L. (1998). Through the lens of giftedness. *Roeper Review, 20,* 204–210.

6

Sensitivity and Empathy for Others

In Dabrowski's Theory of Emotional Development, Level V individuals live a life in service to humanity, and their lives reflect the compassion and forgiveness that represent the core of their being. They are responsible, autonomous, and empathetic. Gifted students manifest a sensitivity and empathy for others early in their development, and their parents and teachers notice this characteristic when they cry easily over stories that are read to them. They are troubled and worried about Peter Rabbit and his dangerous adventures with the farmer. When another child is scolded in their class, it is not uncommon for gifted children to become quite troubled by the distress the other student is feeling. In the context of Dabrowski's theory, this emotional intensity can be viewed as a positive characteristic. Michael Piechowski, a colleague of Dabrowski at the University of Alberta who was responsible for translating much of Dabrowski's work, said emotional intensity is positively correlated with intelligence. The higher the intellectual level, the more emotionally intense a gifted child will be (Piechowski, 2002). If gifted children do not understand that their emotional intensity and heightened sensitivity are normal for them, they may feel and think something is wrong with them. In addition, their teachers may mistake the sensitivity of gifted students as emotional immaturity, rather than what Piechowski calls a rich inner life (Piechowski, 2006).

In this chapter, we address sensitivity and empathy for others as characteristics of gifted students. These two characteristics are reflected in Dabrowski's Theory of Emotional Development in Level V. The feelings of helplessness that gifted students feel concerning the suffering of others is addressed, and ways to alleviate this sense of helplessness are discussed, with an example of eighth grade students responding with empathy to the suffering of animals. A number of activities are introduced that can further develop and maintain sensitivity and empathy including: Care Pairs, Journaling, Identify Your Helpers, Perspective Taking, and Activism.

EMPATHY FOR THE SUFFERING OF OTHERS

Joan Smutny (1998), author and advocate for gifted education from National-Louis University in Evanston, Illinois, said that gifted children sense the joys, pains, sorrows, and hopes of family members, friends, and classmates, and they often are quite distressed when they cannot solve the problems of others. Gifted children are particularly sensitive to cruelty to animals. Albert Schweitzer as a young boy was seldom included in the games of the neighborhood boys, who were rough and cruel to animals. One of their favorite things was to use slingshots to kill birds. In an effort to "be one of the boys," Albert took his slingshot and headed toward the woods with a group of the boys to kill birds. As he got closer to the birds, he suddenly ran ahead of the group, and began shouting and waving his arms to scare the birds away. Of course, they turned on him and pelted him soundly, but he recounts in his autobiography that the incident represented the first time that he vowed to never harm an animal. It was reported that at his hospital in Africa he would walk around a line of ants rather than disturb or step on them (Schweitzer, 1944).

Feelings of Helplessness

Gifted children are bombarded with the daily news of tragedy and suffering throughout the nation and the world, and they keenly feel the suffering of others. Yet, they know they can do nothing about these problems. Consequently, gifted children who are sensitive and empathetic may have deep feelings of helplessness. Harry Passow, former professor at Teachers College in New York City and past president of the World Council for Gifted and Talented, said in his president's address at their conference in Sydney, Australia, that gifted students need to feel equipped to use their talents toward the resolution of global problems. He suggested this could be accomplished by exploring some of the world's problems in social studies and science in problem-based projects, which would help alleviate some of their sense of helplessness (Passow, 1988).

Jim Delisle, a teacher trainer and author of numerous articles and books on gifted education, stressed in *Guiding the Social and Emotional Development of Gifted Children* that today's generation of children is the first in history to receive news about the world crises at the same time as world leaders. He said with the flash of a news bulletin, undigested raw material concerning issues and global problems is put before the eyes and minds of gifted children, who may be left on their own to consider its ramifications (Delisle, 1992).

CASE STUDY

One example of how a teacher can help alleviate this sense of helplessness recently occurred in Mr. Vincent's eighth grade advanced section of biology. Audrey shared with the class that she had heard a news bulletin on the radio (NPR) and then again on the evening television news about the brutal killing of gorillas in the Republic of Congo. She said the alpha male had been shot, along with a pregnant female and another female. Audrey was so distressed over these killings for no apparent reason that her voice quavered, and she visibly shook. Mr. Vincent encouraged Audrey and the other students to go on the Internet to research the number and function of the game preserves, as well as the efforts that the Republic of Congo was making to help ensure that the gorilla population not become endangered or harmed.

Several students agreed to work with Audrey, and they asked if they could work together to prepare a PowerPoint presentation for the class. The following day, the five students who worked with Audrey shared the information they had found: (1) the alarmingly few rangers available to patrol the area, (2) the tremendous loss of forest cleared for subsistence farming, and (3) the apparent apathy of the government. Audrey said, "We've been studying the relationship of man to the environment in our science class, and that environment was theirs; what can we do about this?" Audrey's question resulted in a heated discussion of the need to preserve the environment, and the students began to suggest ideas on ways they could be of assistance to help alleviate the problem. Their ideas included:

1. Write to the embassy of the Republic of Congo to protest the killing of gorillas.

2. Contact the TV stations to see what "stand" they are taking.

3. Contact the Houston Zoo to see what information they have about gorillas.

4. Identify projects they could carry out to raise money to send to the park rangers.

5. Find out if the United States could help or is helping.

6. Find out what the United Nations is doing or could do to help.

IMPORTANCE OF ENABLING GIFTED STUDENTS TO NURTURE THEIR SENSITIVITY AND EMPATHY

It is vitally important that teachers discuss and help gifted students explore the world's problems and possible solutions. In Mr. Vincent's class, Audrey's sensitivity and empathy for the brutal killing of the gorillas became a vehicle or "teaching moment" for the class to explore the problem, and to further develop their concern, personal responsibility, and commitment to be stewards of the earth. The concern, fear, and anxiety that Audrey and the students experienced over this incident evolved into a real-life learning activity for them to address the science standard of *Man's Interaction with the Environment*, which was a *far cry* from just reading about endangered species in the science text.

Benefits of Problem-Based Projects

1. Nurture social consciousness.

2. Stimulate concern for problems.

3. Develop personal responsibility.

4. Encourage commitment to resolve problems.

ACTIVITIES TO DEVELOP AND MAINTAIN EMPATHY

Care Pairs

This activity can be carried out in a number of ways to develop and maintain empathy in the classroom. Gifted children, with their keen sense of empathy for others, will enjoy this activity, and the students who need to develop empathic relationships with others or with nature will also benefit from the experience. First, the teacher would pair the children in dyads and ask them to draw a picture or write or tell a story about something they like very much, or students could bring in an object to share with the class. Then the pairs can talk about the picture, object, or story and the experience behind it. To make sure Care Pairs is an effective strategy, it is important for the teacher to provide enough time for the students to fully share their feelings.

CASE STUDY

Josh, a very sensitive second grade student, brought in a flea collar and said it belonged to Mitzie his pet cat that had been run over and killed. The youngster began to softly cry, and Zack, his care pair partner, told about the death of his dog and how unhappy he had been. The boys talked softly, as if they instinctively wanted to privately experience the feelings in their dyad, and they talked about taking care of their pets. Miss Ward, the teacher noticed that after this experience, Zack and Josh sought one another out for games and for school work. She knows the death of a pet can be devastating for anyone, but particularly for young children. Miss Ward extended the care pair lesson by having the children go outside, where she asked them to imagine how a tree, bird, rock, squirrel, caterpillar or other parts of nature would "feel" if it were treated well. Then she asked them to imagine that they were a part of nature and to demonstrate with a verbal response something that would please that living thing or object.

Jason said, "I am a caterpillar, and when the boy picked me up, I was scared he would hurt me. He looked at me real close and then put me down. I am so happy." Marta said, "I am a flower, and when you pulled the weed next to me, that was nice. I have more room." Miguel said, "I am a tree. When you picked up litter around me, that was good—I hated looking at it."

The last two responses indicate that the children identified with the flower and the tree, and they were speaking to the class from that viewpoint. Through such simple activities, Miss Ward was able to strengthen the concept of empathic relationships. Teachable moments often spontaneously happen, and sensitive and skillful teachers can use them to engage their students in meaningful activities. Miss Ward shared with the children in her class that the earth is "home" for all of its creatures. She said, "We call this a *habitat*, the place where people, plants, and animals live, and we need to be stewards of the earth." At this point, Miss Ward asked, "Do any of you know what a steward does? Marta, who is probably the "biophile" of the class with a strong affinity to nature, said, "Does it mean help the earth?" Jason said, "Be kind to the earth." Miss Ward acknowledged both responses and said, "A steward does both of those things, helping and being kind to the earth." Miss Ward then suggested the students go back to the classroom and said, "I have a wonderful book for your story time: *The Giving Tree* by Shel Silverstein." She made eye contact with Miguel who had spoken from the point of view of a tree.

Journaling

Journaling is one of the better ways to gain insight into one's self, and gifted students can experience the sensory observations typically found in the notebooks of scientists, explorers, writers, and artists. The private and the personal nature of journaling makes it a perfect tool to encourage spontaneous expression and discovery. The journal is a safe place for gifted students to be themselves, to feel, think, observe, and dream. As long as the journal is kept confidential, except for selective sharing when students indicate that they would like to share something from their journal, the only criticism that the students face is self-criticism. For gifted students, this may be a real obstacle for keeping a journal; however, encouraging the addition of drawings in a journal can open up the process of self-understanding, and adding color further enhances the journaling process.

One problem that many gifted students have is finding a support system to provide them the understanding, honest feedback, encouragement, support, and assistance they need when their empathy and sensitivity is misunderstood, devalued, or ignored. Writing in their journals can help gifted students understand that sometimes you need to reach out for assistance. Teachers, guidance counselors, and parents can suggest topics for gifted students to journal, such as the identification of helpers, or the students can journal on their own with whatever interests them.

Identify Your Helpers

In this exercise suggested by Lucia Capacchione (1989) in *The Well-Being Journal,* students are guided to identify people they can turn to when they need assistance. These individuals can be family members, friends, neighbors, or professionals who provide special services such as a guidance counselor, physician, or minister. The teacher can say:

> Consider the people who provide you help when you need it, and see them in your mind's eye. What do they do to support you? Identify ways that you support them. Now hold this picture in your mind. In your journal, draw a circle that represents you, and then draw smaller circles for those who support you. Journal your thoughts about your need for help and assistance, and identify your support system.

Tyrone, who is 16, drew a circle in his journal and quickly drew seven circles. He included his mom, dad, brother Jarrod, and sister Cece. Then he added Baylor, a classmate of his from elementary school through tenth grade; his minister, the Reverend Mr. Thomas; and his basketball coach, Mr. Lee. In his journal Tyrone wrote:

> When I think of the people who help me, I first thought of my family. If anyone in our family has a problem, we can bring it up at supper and everyone dives in and gives ideas. And in my mind's eye, I saw how I felt when I didn't make the varsity team and the new coach's criticism of my playing hurt so much. He looked right through me, and said I wasn't on the varsity team. I felt like a little kid—I almost cried in front of the team. But Baylor helped me by saying he knew how I felt, and he wished that I had been chosen for varsity instead of him. Later in church, the minister talked about "humbling yourself" and I realized that I had felt like a hot shot and I didn't always work with the team—I hogged the ball! I took too many risk shots. It is hard for me to write this, but now I know how other people feel when things don't go the way they would hope. I'm going to ask the coach, Mr. Lee, to help me be a better player. Baylor said we would plan some one-on-one, and that is always fun and it would help both of us be better team players.

Through journaling about his support system, Tyrone identified a number of people who could or did give him assistance, and he began to use his own empathy to think about how other people don't always have things turn out the way they would hope. He also demonstrated his sensitivity in being part of a team, as he reflected on how he did or did not work with the team.

Modeling

Modeling empathy is a powerful strategy for teachers and parents to use. For example, when you read a book to a class or to your children in which one of the characters is left out of a party, you could pause and comment on how sad and lonely she must feel. Or as you stand in the line behind an elderly person in the grocery line, searching for change, you could smile at him or her and allow your children to observe your empathy and patience. Or when a car in front of you is going slowly, you might suggest that the driver could be a student driver and share how you felt when you were first learning how to drive. Still another opportunity to model empathy is when someone is talking in a very loud voice; you might suggest that the person may have a hearing problem.

CASE STUDY

Empathy and sensitivity to others is one of the major areas of focus in a summer residential leadership program for high school gifted students at Lamar University. Recently, when the students were attending a musical of *The King & I* at a junior college, an older couple slowly shuffled down the aisle in the dark trying to find a seat, blocking a major part of the stage. Suddenly, one of the students in the leadership program, Justin, stood up and asked if he could help them find a seat. He found two seats and quickly came back to his own seat. This simple gesture of sensitivity was a model for the other students and provided an opportunity for Justin to spontaneously demonstrate his empathy. On the way home on the school bus, the students talked about his act of empathy, and Justin said, "I would hope someone would help me when I need it, and I know how it feels to be confused." With this comment, he verbally identified the core of empathy: placing yourself in the other person's shoes.

Perspective Taking

David Johnson (2003) in *Reaching Out: Interpersonal Effectiveness and Self-Actualization* emphasized the importance of taking the other person's perspective and expressing empathy for him or her. He defined perspective-taking and empathy as ways to seek to help others and to avoid harming them, to the extent that we can imagine being in their position. This process of perspective-taking would ask students to treat the ideas of others respectfully and nonjudgmentally, as well as to accept individuals for who they are.

One important aspect of perspective-taking is to develop an appreciation for the historic, cultural, ethnic, and religious backgrounds of others. Johnson emphasized the need to reflect on whether ethnocentricity is inherent in one's definition of self. He discussed the development of an in-group identity that does not lead to a rejection of out-groups. He identified examples of groups in which you must reject other groups to belong, such as the Ku Klux Klan and the Boy Scouts of America.

Johnson suggested that students research their own cultural heritage, and then find someone in their class with similar cultural heritage. Then he suggested that students with similar cultural backgrounds plan a presentation that could include the following:

- Definition of cultural identity (Who are we?)
- History of culture (What is our history?)
- Traditions of cultures (What are our traditions?)
- Aspects of culture food, songs, and art (Examples of our culture . . .)
- Personal experiences as a member of the culture (My personal experiences as a member of this culture . . . (Johnson, 2003, p. 351)

A tenth grade student working with a perspective-taking activity in his history class had the following to say:

Finding out about other cultures was awesome. Where I live most people are all alike, and studying different cultures—their food, music, dance, and art—was great. These differences or diversity make life much more interesting, and I was amazed at how similar we are, as well as different. I want to walk in all of their shoes.

Activism for Young People

Phil Hoose (1993) in *It's Our World Too: Stories of Young People Who Are Making a Difference* included a section on activism for young people. He suggested that students who want to make a difference follow six steps:

1. Choose a project you really care about.

2. Find others to work with.

3. Write a vision statement.

4. Keep adults from taking over.

5. Conduct research.

6. Create a working plan.

The book includes specific tools for change-making, such as how to write a letter, use a petition to build support, use the media, ask for money and other support, conduct a boycott, lobby, protest, and demonstrate (Hoose, 1993). Teachers can use these steps to help their gifted students select a project that will be meaningful to them and further build and develop their sensitivity and empathy for others.

EXAMPLES OF ACTIVISM DEMONSTRATING SENSITIVITY AND EMPATHY

Mara Sapon-Shevin (1999) in *Because We Can Change the World* tells about a first grade teacher in Amherst, Massachusetts, who worked with her students to advocate having an arrow removed from the Pilgrim's hat symbol on the Massachusetts Turnpike signs. The students talked about how insensitive it was to imply that the Native Americans attacked the Pilgrims. They wrote letters to the local newspaper, to the governor, and to the state representatives about the issue. The result was the turnpike sign was changed and the first grade students found out that they could make a difference (Sapon-Shevin, 1999).

Another example of student activism involved two 16-year-old students—a Hispanic football player, Neto Villareal, the star running back, and a white, student leader, Andy Percifield—who challenged racism on the football field in Idaho. During games, the fans would yell racist comments about the Hispanic players on the football team, who made up about 50 percent of the team. The Hispanic players considered quitting the team, but they didn't want to be perceived as quitters. Neto and his friend Jesse, another Hispanic football player, approached Andy, the student leader and asked him to talk to the principal. The principal denied there was a problem and refused to get involved. Neto spoke to the school board and told them what was happening at the games. Then Andy drafted a letter, ran off 100 copies, and called together a meeting of all the student body. When the students gathered, he explained the issue of racism being demonstrated in the games and read them the letter he had written:

> We, the student body of Marsing High School, are appalled at the racist behavior of certain people in the audience. Not only does this set a bad example for younger students, it also reflects very badly on our entire school and community. Although we appreciate the support of our fans for our team, which is comprised of students from many ethnic backgrounds, we do not need bigots here. We are asking the authorities to reject from the premises anyone making such rude and racist remarks.
>
> Marsing High School Student Body

The students passed out copies of the letter to everyone at the game, and a member of the student council read the letter aloud at half-time. Almost everyone stood up and cheered. Neto said, "We made it known that we wouldn't accept racism in our school or from our fans. We made a difference in the part of our lives that we really could control" (Hoose, 1993).

These examples are exciting because the students saw a situation that needed to be changed, and they used their sensitivity to the issue and their empathy for the individuals who were being treated unfairly or an implication of their behavior that was not true, to make a difference. Rather than leaving the students feeling frustrated and feeling helpless about the situations, they could actively participate in bringing about a solution to the problems.

SUMMARY

This chapter addressed sensitivity and empathy for others that are characteristics of gifted students. These two characteristics are reflected in Dabrowski's Theory of Emotional Development in Level V in which individuals spend their lives in service to humanity, and their lives reflect the compassion and forgiveness that represent the core of their being. They are responsible, autonomous, and empathetic. Gifted students are emotionally intense, and Piechowski (2002) said the higher the intellectual level, the more emotionally intense a gifted child will be.

Gifted students have empathy for the suffering of others, and they can also have feelings of helplessness as they are exposed to global issues and crises. An example of a way of alleviating this sense of helplessness was provided by an eighth grade science class that became involved in a problem-based project over the brutal killing of gorillas in the Republic of Congo. The importance of enabling gifted students to nurture their sensitivity and empathy was discussed and the benefits of problem-based projects were listed.

Activities to develop and maintain sensitivity and empathy for others were identified and discussed including Care Pairs with a case study of second grade students using this strategy. Journaling was discussed as an activity in which gifted students can experience the sensory observations typically found in the notebooks of scientists, explorers, writers, and artists. Identify Your Helpers, Perspective Taking, and Activism for students were discussed as activities to further develop the gifted students' sensitivity and empathy for others, Examples of student activism at the first grade level and at the high school level were provided. These activities rather than leaving gifted students feeling helpless about problems, encouraged them to become actively involved in bringing about solutions, and turning their sensitivity and empathy for others into positive enabling characteristics.

Teacher Voice

I did not realize that sensitivity and empathy were characteristics of a gifted child. Now that I know, I understand more why things happen the way they do with my gifted students. In my classroom, I discourage insensitivity to others. I can speak personally about how cruel people can be from my childhood days. I have a student who is handicapped in my class this year, and my gifted students are so empathetic to him, they worry if he falls, and they help him up, and, if he needs help getting something off the floor, they always help. They even make sure that he gets his lunch tray to the table safely. They constantly remind him to "slow down." Gifted children need to understand that their emotional intensity and heightened sensitivity are normal for them. I use journaling in my class, and that helps them share their feelings. I plan to use the Care Pairs idea in my class to get my students actively involved in solutions. It would work very well with any of our project-based activities in science or social studies. My class is very interested in environmental issues, especially as they affect animals—I guess that is their sensitivity being displayed.

Shaelyn Anderson
Science teacher, fifth grade

Read On

Cooper, C. (2007). I'm a kid, mom, not a robot: What high ability children want their parents to know about them. *Parenting for High Potential,* (June), 18–20.

Delisle, J. (2000). *Once upon a mind: The stories and scholars of gifted child education.* Belmont, CA: Wadsworth.

Dunton, S. (2006). Building microsociety. *Education Leadership, 63*(8), 86–90.

Helm, J., & Katz, L. (2001). *Young investigators: The project approach in the early years.* New York: Teachers College Press.

Lee, K. (2007). Joseph. *Gifted Child Today, 30*(2), 40–41.

Log On

Discovery Education School Resources Site (http://school.discoveryeducation.com/). This Discovery Channel Web site includes rubrics for evaluating student performance on project-based learning.

EcoKids Online (http://ecokids.earthday.ca/). This site offers information about the environment through games and activities. Children are encouraged to get involved and understand what effects their own actions have on the environment.

Women's Adventures in Science (http://www.iwaswondering.org/). Provides scrapbooks, videos, and interactive cartoons to build empathy for the unique role of women in science.

Reflect On

- Do students willingly share their strengths and weaknesses with one another in a sensitive and supportive atmosphere? If not, why not?
- What is the message in Shel Silverstein's book *The Giving Tree?* How empathetic and sensitive was the boy? And can we be too giving?
- In our growing diverse population, developing students' empathy and sensitivity becomes of great importance. What can be done to teach tolerance? Do you think you can teach tolerance?
- Steven Cozza, a Boy Scout in Petaluma, California, at the age of 12 started *Scouting for All* to end discrimination against gays by the Boy Scouts because he felt offended by their policy of excluding gays from becoming members of Boy Scouts. What do you think?

REFERENCES

Capacchione, L. (1989). *The well-being journal.* Hollywood, CA: Newcastle.

Cooper, C. (2007). I'm a kid, mom, not a robot: What high ability children want their parents to know about them. *Parenting for High Potential,* (June), 18–20.

Delisle, J. (1992). *Guiding the social and emotional development of gifted children.* New York: Longman.

Delisle, J. (2000). *Once upon a mind: The stories and scholars of gifted child education.* Belmont, CA: Wadsworth.

Dunton, S. (2006). Building microsociety. *Education Leadership, 63*(8), 86–90.

Helm, J., & Katz, L. (2001). *Young investigators: The project approach in the early years.* New York: Teachers College Press.

Hoose, P. (1993). *It's our world too: Stories of young people who are making a difference.* Boston: Little & Brown.

Johnson, D. (2003). *Reaching out: Interpersonal effectiveness and self-actualization.* Boston: Allyn & Bacon.

Lee, K. (2007). Joseph. *Gifted Child Today, 30*(2), 40–41.

Passow, A. H. (1988, August). Presidential address at the World Conference for Gifted and Talented in Sidney, Australia.

Piechowski, M. (2002). Experiencing in a higher key: Dabrowski's theory of and for the gifted. *Communicator, 33*(1), 31–36.

Piechowski, M. (2006). *Mellow out they say, if only I could: Intensities and sensitiveness of the young and bright.* Madison, WI: Yunasa Books.

Sapon-Shevin, M. (1999). *Because we can change the world.* Boston: Allyn & Bacon.

Schweitzer, A. (1944). *Out of my life and thought.* New York: Holt.

Smutny, J. (1998). Recognizing and honoring the sensitivities of gifted children. *Communicator, 29*(3) 10–11.

7

Reflective Thinking

You Are in Charge

Reflective thinking is thinking about your thinking and what you are thinking about. Webster's unabridged dictionary defines *reflect* as to think seriously, contemplate, and to ponder. When you engage in reflective thinking, you step outside of your self and become an observer: What are you thinking? What are you feeling? How do your thoughts and feelings affect your behavior? Being in charge means you are responsible for your attitudes and how you react to everything in your life, and most importantly, you have a choice between being positive or negative, regardless of what is going on around you. It is possible to have absolute peace, dignity, and some joy in your life in the most miserable of circumstances. An example of this can be noted in the behavior of Holocaust victims who created plays and cabarets, wrote sonatas, and nurtured one another in the midst of a "living hell on earth" (Frankl, 1957). Yet, it is also possible to have agony, anger, and sorrow in your life in the best of circumstances, depending on how you choose your attitudes.

CHANGING YOUR THINKING

One helpful concept in tackling the idea of changing your thinking is the notion of "being in the moment" in order to experience reality. Ram Dass (2000), former professor at Princeton University and leader in human development workshops, said that most of us are wrapped up in our own personal soap opera, or what he called the "mellow drama" of who we think we are, and we carry our past with us. Our thoughts are tied to our emotions, and we feel exactly the way we think. The following story was shared with me by Wyman Ainsley, a creativity and wellness specialist. The story illustrates the importance of letting go of the past.

Two monks were walking down a muddy street through a small village. They saw a young woman in a beautiful kimono on one side of the street who was obviously wondering how she could cross over to the other side. One of the two monks went over, picked her up and carried her across the street.

They walked on and the second monk didn't say anything. Finally that evening he could stand it no longer, so about that beautiful woman he said, "We monks aren't supposed to go near beautiful women, say nothing of carrying them across the street!"

The first monk said, "Are you still carrying her? I put her down in the marketplace this morning."

This story illustrates the importance of not carrying past hurts or experiences around. By reflecting on this story, you can begin to discover the power of your thoughts. Thoughts determine our actions, attitudes, and self-image. If you dwell on depressing or negative thoughts concerning the past, you will experience a negative and depressing life today. Negative thoughts are like a magnet—you will tend to move toward negative people, activities, philosophies, and life styles. Our life follows our thoughts, if we think positive, happy, joyful thoughts, we will attract other happy, upbeat positive people into our life. Thoughts are tied to our emotions—we feel exactly the way we think. As we think happy thoughts, we begin to feel the way we think.

The Brain Is Like a Computer

Think of your brain as a huge computer that stores everything you know and everything you have experienced. When you think positive, creative thoughts, you are moving toward greatness. It is important to continually choose to keep your mind on higher things, no matter what happens to you. If you look hard enough, you can find something good about any experience. In the annual summer workshops of the Creative Problem Solving Institute in Buffalo, New York, there is an exercise used to help the participants focus on positive thoughts. The participants are asked to try to think of something bad that has happened to them, and then to think what is good about that?

For example, let's say you broke your leg. What's good about that? (1) You get a rest, (2) people feel sorry for you, (3) people will take care of you, (4) you have time to read lots of books that you have wanted to read, and (5) people will write nice things on your cast. No matter what you are going through, if you look hard enough, you can find something good about the situation. You just have to stay focused and be positive. By choosing your thoughts and focusing on the positive, you can reprogram your computer.

Thoughts Are Tied to Emotions

The following activity will stimulate gifted students to become more reflective. Ask them to find a quiet place and jot down the first idea that comes to mind after reflecting on the following prompts:

When I think of happiness, I think of

_____

_____

_____

I feel happy when I find myself feeling

_____

_____

_____

I am happy when I am doing

_____

_____

_____

CASE STUDY

When Shaniqua, age 16, was given an opportunity to reflect on the three prompts by her counselor, she wrote, "When I think of happiness, I think of being with my family, laughing with them, and being loved." Responding to the second prompt, she noted, "I am happy when I feel safe and appreciated by my family, by my friends, and by my teachers. For the third prompt, she wrote, "I am happy when I am doing what I know is best for me and others."

Shaniqua added, "By reflecting on happiness, I couldn't help but think what makes me unhappy. It's when I feel that people don't understand me, appreciate me, or even like me." Her counselor nodded, and asked, "What do you do when you think and feel that way?" Shaniqua quickly responded. "I try to get as far away from those people as possible, and I shut down." The counselor continued, "What if you have those feelings and thoughts in school?" Shaniqua said, "I don't answer, I don't volunteer, and my mind is on hold."

The Computer as a Metaphor for the Brain

Shaniqua is not unusual with her thinking, feeling, and acting. Most gifted students thrive in situations in which they feel the teachers like them and their classmates see them as valued members of the class. When this isn't the case, it is helpful for gifted students to think of the computer as a metaphor for their brain. As a computer, the brain holds all of the information, experiences, thoughts, feelings, and past behavior of each one of us. In some cases, it is important for gifted students to learn to reprogram their computer.

Reprogramming Your Mental Computer

One technique to use in reprogramming your computer is to use affirmations. For example, let's say someone tells you that you are a lousy dancer and that you have no rhythm. You might use this affirmation, "Every day I am becoming more and more of a great dancer." Repeat this affirmation throughout the day, and even write it on a piece of paper and tape it on your bathroom mirror. Soon you will become the dancer that your friends and classmates said you weren't. Or, let's say someone claims that you are not helpful. An affirmation would be, "Every day I am becoming more and more helpful." Saying, thinking, and reflecting on this affirmation places it in your mental computer. Affirmations are a powerful technique because our thoughts have tremendous power, and we tend to draw into our lives what we think about.

Other affirmations might include, "Every day I am becoming more and more of a computer expert." It is important to point out that affirmations are worded in a similar fashion to the developmental nature in the Dabrowski Theory of Emotional Development, in that we are all in the process of reaching toward our ideal self, rather than thinking that it will happen immediately. Emotions follow our thoughts, and they influence our actions and our behavior. This concept was illustrated in Chapter 5 with the awareness of self model, which explains how we gather information from our sensory perceptions and reflect upon this information through interpretive thought, which in turn activates our emotions that impact and influence our desires, intentions, and wills, and finally results in our behaviors and action.

Given this model, it is clear that it's important to choose to see the bright optimistic side of life, no matter what you are going through. If you look hard enough, you can find something good about any situation. You just have to stay focused and be positive.

STRATEGIES TO ENCOURAGE REFLECTIVE THINKING

Making Connections

Reflective thinking involves making connections, and one strategy that teachers can use is to place the following activity on the board before the students arrive, or on a handout for them to work on before class begins.

Think about

Think of a sound and write it down. _____

Now think of a smell and write it down. _____

Think of something you touch and write it down. _____

Think of something you taste and write it down. _____

Think of something you have seen and write it down. _____

Think of something you have done and write it down. _____

Now finish these prompts

Sounds like this make me think of _____.

Smells like this make me think of _____.

Touching this makes me think of _____.

Tasting this makes me think of _____.

Seeing this makes me think of _____.

Doing this makes me think of _____.

Chloe, a fifth grade gifted student, gleefully grabbed the handout and began writing her responses. She identified the sound as a burp from her baby sister; the smell was the sweet, powdery smell of the baby; touching was the smooth skin of the baby's foot; tasting was the hot chocolate her mother makes when she comes home from school; seeing was the *100* she saw on her math paper; and doing was learning her lines in the class play, *A Midsummer's Night Dream*.

Chloe's response sheet captured her reflective thinking and her shift in thinking from home to school:

Sounds like this make me think of my baby sister Sara's burp.

Smells like this make me think of the powdery smell of Sara.

Touching this makes me think of the soft skin of her foot.

Tasting this makes me think of how good hot chocolate is when I get home from school.

Seeing this makes me think of how cool that 100 was in mathematics.

Doing this makes me proud I have a part in the school play.

After Chloe finished the prompts, she said, "What a great way to get my brain to start thinking this morning. Are we going to share these?" Each student comes to school with his or her life—a living, dynamic life—and opportunities to reflect on that life helps them to see the connections they have with others, with their school, and with their community. When students are provided opportunities to reflect, the next step is to provide time for them to share with one another, which will help build a community of your learners. School can become like a fan, opening up to more and more things, leading to bigger and bigger things.

Reflecting on Appearance

Appearance is vitally important to all adolescents, and gifted adolescents can be excessively critical of others, as well as of themselves. The following activity was used with a group of high school gifted students to help them reflect on their attitudes concerning appearances. The teacher gave the group the following list and asked them to write *pleasing* or *offensive* by each word or phrase.

Appearance

Clean	Fat
Long hair	Short
Neat	Skinny
Messy	Dirty
Freckled	Hand-me-downs
Ugly	Missing teeth
Smelly	Strong perfume
Strong cologne	Runny nose

After the group of students wrote *pleasing* or *offensive* by each word or phrase, they began to discuss the exercise. One student said, "I don't think it is right to say something is offensive if the person can't help being short, having a runny nose, or missing teeth." Another student, quickly responded, "But you don't have to be messy, dirty, or smelly, and that is offensive." As the students shared their responses and comments, you could see how reflective they had become in thinking about their judgments. One student remarked, "I learned a great deal about myself in this activity, and some kids like me have to wear hand-me-downs." At which point, another student said, "If I had hand-me-downs as nice as yours are, that would be no problem."

As they left the room, students were still talking about the exercise and sharing with one another why they had made their decision to call items pleasing or offensive. The teacher later observed, "In our increasingly complex world, the thinking process has become essential in the learning process, and in this activity reflecting on their values and attributes was quite productive for my students, as they move toward respecting the individuality of people, and in demonstrating empathy for others." In this observation, the teacher is also reflecting on her teaching, and demonstrating sensitivity to the diversity of the needs and backgrounds of her students. Reflective thinking for the teacher involved self-monitoring of her satisfaction with the effectiveness of the activity, and the growth she noted in her students' ability to reflect on their attitudes and behavior concerning appearance.

Conditions that need to be addressed in encouraging meaningful reflective thinking for students include the following:

1. Students need to feel safe about what they think.

2. Reflective activities should be meaningful.

3. Reflective questions, prompts, and responses should be specific.

4. Reflective thinking needs to be modeled by teachers and parents.

Reflective Prompts for School Assignments

Gifted students often set such high standards for themselves that they are never satisfied with their learning. Reflective thinking can help gifted students to describe how they see themselves as students, and how well they perform as students on specific lessons or projects. A reflective prompt could include the following.

Check the appropriate description of your work

___ I feel good about this assignment.

___ I am proud of this work.

___ I put forth my best effort.

___ I enjoyed doing this assignment.

___ I met my goals.

___ I could have done a lot better.

___ It wasn't my best work.

___ I didn't put much effort into this assignment.

___ I didn't reach my goals.

BENEFITS OF REFLECTIVE THINKING

The more gifted students use their reflective thinking, the better they will become in understanding themselves not only as learners, but as individuals with strengths and weaknesses. Art Costa and Bena Kallick (2005) compared schooling to a spaceship launchpad, with all the life-support systems remaining attached to the command center until the moment of liftoff, when the spaceship is suddenly on its own. They made the case that students are launched from school into life, internalizing the lessons they have learned in school. They advocated self-direction, self-managing, self-monitoring, and self-modifying behaviors for success in life. Reflection is needed to develop these skills, and teachers can ask students to reflect on their knowledge, skills, attitudes, and dispositions.

Giselle Martin-Kniep (2000) in *Becoming a Better Teacher: Eight Innovations That Work* stressed that students can evaluate the merits and shortcomings of their products, processes, or performances, and provide reflective feedback to their teachers on their lessons and units of study by communicating what they have learned and experienced.

CASE STUDY

Caitland is in an honors English class in which the students were asked to select a project to work on that would provide them opportunities to use their creative writing skills. Caitland decided to write about Hildegarde de Bingen, an eleventh-century nun. She turned in her paper and received an A. However, when she was asked to reflect on her work, she made a connection between her original intent to blend her love of music, particularly that of the flute, and her research paper. Her self-assessment follows.

Missed the Mark

I am not pleased with my final product, even though researching Hildegarde de Bingen was a great experience. She was truly a phenomenal woman and her music is still played today. I listened to several pieces and tried unsuccessfully to transpose a couple of pieces to play on my flute. That just didn't work. The paper was to be limited to ten pages, and mine was ten pages, but there was so much more I wanted to say about her, her influence on the Catholic Church, and on the nuns she worked with as mother superior. She had unbelievable people skills, and she could criticize the church and still be recognized as a leader in the church. She was so funny and practical, she allowed the nuns to drink beer because the quality of the water was so bad, and she said it made their cheeks rosy.

I listened to the other oral reports and they were interesting, but my topic person touched my life, and I couldn't write about that because of the time constraint, or maybe because of my lack of organization in my writing. I now know I should have stepped back from the report and outlined what I wanted to say and why. I wanted to talk about her influence on current music and her incredible courage to be who she was. Our oral reports were limited to ten minutes and I used three minutes playing one of her CDs, which was dumb. When I realized how much material I had, and the limited space, I just wrote it to get it done. I'm glad we had this assignment, I learned so much about Hildegarde de Bingen and her incredible faith, but I am/was very unhappy about my final project. I needed more flexibility in presenting the topic, and more time.

Caitland's teacher was somewhat surprised about her reflection on the project. He had graded the project as an A and was impressed with her references, and the fact that she had located a CD of the music of Hildegarde de Bingen. The students had asked lots of questions and Caitland answered them with accurate information, appearing highly responsive. After reading her reflection, he decided to provide a number of options for future work in his class, such as background papers with historical research emphasis, creative papers in which the students could focus on what they learned about their eminent individual, and implementation papers in which the focus would be on how the person's life and contribution affected future generations. He recognized that it would have been helpful to Caitland to have had opportunities to talk with him on the progress of her report throughout the semester. Therefore, he decided to provide ongoing time for the students to share what they were finding out about their individual. Last, he stressed that he wanted to ensure that his students become engaged in rich tasks involving strategic planning and creative approaches. The challenge for teachers is to challenge their students to engage in a variety of authentic rich tasks (Moulds, 2004).

Importance of Reflective Activities

Teachers need to provide their students opportunities to reflect on their work on a regular basis. The more opportunities gifted students have to reflect, the better understanding they can build of themselves as learners and as unique individuals. Reflection encourages honest feedback between teachers and students. Caitland's response to the teacher's three choices for a paper was, "I wanted to do all three, but I see now that was my problem. I need to focus and prioritize." She said laughingly, "Or write a book."

SELF-EFFICACY

Self-efficacy can be defined as having the power to be effective, and reflective thinking is a natural partner for gifted students to become more self-effective. A checklist to measure whether a student has developed self-efficacy was developed in an early program for the gifted in Garden Grove, California, by a group of teachers who wanted their gifted students to be self-regulated learners. The checklist was highly effective in providing feedback to the teachers and to the gifted students who reflected on being workers/learners in individual and group projects.

In this class I am . . .

____Enjoying working on my projects

____Using my imagination in identifying projects and products

____Challenged by my projects

____Working on a project that is involved with "real-life"

_____Interested in what I am researching

_____Excited about working on my project

_____Satisfied with my work on my project

Reflective thinking is learner-centered, and for it to be used effectively, students need time to reflect. Gifted students, with their critical nature, enjoy reflecting on their knowledge, skills, attitudes, and dispositions, and they are capable of evaluating the merits of their work, including the processes as well as the products. Reflective thinking enables gifted students to examine their learning and encourages them to be more in charge of their learning. The checklist above can also be used for large-group discussion with an entire class, in which the students are asked to reflect on and discuss the different lessons that they experience. Reflective teachers think about what is happening in their classes, as well as how they can improve the learning opportunities for their students. The same self-monitoring that gifted students demonstrate with their critical nature can be accomplished by teachers who are reflective and self-monitoring.

DYNAMIC NATURE OF TEACHING

Teaching is not static. It is dynamic and ever-changing, particularly as the student body grows and continues to change, becoming more and more diverse, and the field of knowledge continues to grow exponentially. The reflective student and teacher engaged in reflective teaching and learning will become synergistically involved, for as the gifted students reflect on their experiences and become more self-regulated, their teachers can use this feedback to adapt lessons and the curriculum to become more effective in meeting their unique educational needs. In a sense, today's teachers are moving toward the role of the wise and trusted counselor who is an advisor, teacher, role model, and friend.

SUMMARY

In this chapter, reflective thinking was defined as thinking about your thinking, and what you are thinking about. The notion of gifted students being in charge and being responsible for their attitudes, and how they react to everything in their lives, was discussed, as well as the importance of making choices between being positive or negative in their responses. The idea of changing your thinking was covered with the need to let go of the past. The brain was compared to a computer that stores everything you know and everything you have experienced. The tie between emotions and thoughts was discussed with a case study as an example of a student using reflective thinking. Reprogramming one's mental computer was covered and examples of ways to reprogram your brain, including the use of affirmations were discussed. Strategies to encourage students to reflect on their school work were provided.

The concept of reflective thinking was examined in relation to reflective teaching in which teachers provide opportunities for students to reflect and provide feedback about their learning and the teacher's lessons. The importance of the synergistic nature of reflective thinking and reflective teaching was introduced and the importance of the teacher being an advisor, teacher, role model, and friend was discussed.

Teacher Voice

After reading this chapter, I thought about one of my students, and how much progress he has made. At the first of the year, David would complain that everything was too hard or he would say he couldn't do it. One day after listening to his complaints and seeing the look of frustration on his face, I asked him if football was too hard. Then I asked if he ever said he couldn't do it. David said "no" to both of the questions. Then I told him that every time he said negative comments, his brain processed that information. I stressed that positive thoughts affect our behavior and how we react to situations. When I noticed David starting to get frustrated, I would quietly say to him, "I can do this; this isn't that hard." For the past week, David has not spoken one negative comment. He has been working on reprogramming his "computer" (the brain), and positive encouragement has greatly influenced his actions and behavior.

Teachers need to encourage students to reflect on their thinking so they can better understand themselves and their strengths and weaknesses. Teachers also need to model reflective thinking for their students and provide them opportunities to reflect on their attitudes, knowledge, skills, and disposition. This allows the teachers to better understand their students and their needs, so they can adjust lessons and curriculum appropriately. Reflective thinking is an essential tool for student success throughout their lives. Also, teachers need to use reflective thinking themselves to evaluate their teaching methods and strategies. This year I implemented journals, and it has helped unorganized students be more organized, as well as encouraged creativity and ownership of their work. The role of the teacher has changed throughout the years. Today a teacher wears many hats, and one of them is reflective thinking.

Jennie Knapp
Eighth grade pre-AP teacher

Read On

Cooper, C. (2007). I'm a kid, mom, not a robot: What high-ability children want their parents to know about them. *Parenting for High Potential,* (June), 18–21.

Costa, A., & Kallick, B. (2004). *Assessment strategies for self-directed learning.* Thousand Oaks, CA: Corwin.

Martin-Kniep, G. (2000). *Becoming a better teacher: Eight innovations that work.* Columbus, OH: Merrill Prentice Hall.

Moore, K. (2005). *Effective instructional strategies: From theory to practice.* Thousand Oaks, CA: Sage.

Sapolsky, R. (2004). *Why zebras don't get ulcers.* New York: Henry Holt.

Log On

Association for Experiential Education (http://www.aee.org/). A Web site with resources to make direct hands-on experiences in teaching.

Pro Teacher (http://www.proteacher.com/). A Web site to explore self-monitoring and reflective practices.

Raising Resilient Kids (http://www.raisingresilientkids.com/). A Web site with suggestions on raising resilient kids.

Reflect On

- Think of a school situation in which you were highly motivated to accomplish something. Reflect on the outcome. What motivated you?
- How would you design a happy classroom to encourage your students to keep a positive attitude toward themselves, others, and learning?
- How can teachers teach for meaning? Does reflective teaching provide an answer? In what ways do you see reflective teaching enhancing teaching for meaning?
- Self-managing, self-monitoring, and self-modifying capabilities characterize peak performers in all walks of life. What can we do to develop these skills?

REFERENCES

Cooper, C. (2007). I'm a kid, mom, not a robot: What high-ability children want their parents to know about them. *Parenting for High Potential,* (June), 18–21.

Costa, A., & Kallick, B. (2004). *Assessment strategies for self-directed learning.* Thousand Oaks, CA: Corwin.

Costa, A., & Kallick, B. (2005). Launching self-directed learners. *Educational Leadership, 62*(1), 51–55.

Dass, R. (2000). *Still here.* New York: Penguin.

Frankl, V. (1957). *The doctor and the soul.* New York: Knopf.

Martin-Kniep, G. (2000). *Becoming a better teacher: Eight innovations that work.* Columbus, OH: Merrill Prentice Hall.

Moore, K. (2005). *Effective instructional strategies: From theory to practice.* Thousand Oaks, CA: Sage.

Moulds, P. (2004). Rich tasks. *Educational Leadership, 51*(4), 75–79.

Sapolsky, R. (2004). *Why zebras don't get ulcers.* New York: Henry Holt.

8

Developing Creativity in Gifted Students

Everywhere you look you see the words creative and innovative. All you need to do is to flip through the pages of any magazine said Jim Pierce (1998), a consultant with St. Onge Company, an independent engineering firm, to see page after page of advertisements of creative products and services. What does it mean to be creative and innovative? Are they the same thing? Other questions come to mind, such as are we born creative? Can you develop creativity? Gary Davis (2003), an educator who has spent most of his professional life exploring the answers to the latter question, says "yes" and "yes." That is, some people are born creative and others have had their creativity developed using strategies that Davis and other educators and psychologists, including Sidney Parnes, Doris Shallcross, and E. Paul Torrance, designed to develop creativity.

This chapter examines the definitions of creativity and explores the theory that creativity is a necessary component of giftedness, as posed by Joseph Renzulli (1977) in his TRIAD model, and a second theory as posed by E. Paul Torrance (1962a) that creativity is a unique type of giftedness. This introductory section is followed by ways to identify creativity and a discussion of the variety of instruments being used to identify creative students. In addition, we explore the use of creativity in developing skills in creative problem solving that were planned and implemented in the Creative Problem Solving Institute under the early direction of Alex Osborne (1963) and Sidney Parnes (1981).

DEFINITIONS OF CREATIVITY

Creativity is a complex concept, and there are many definitions from the fields of education, sociology, psychology, and business. James Gallagher, a pioneer in the field of gifted education, and former President of the World Council for Gifted and Talented (WCGT), Assistant Secretary of Education in the division of Health Education and Welfare (HEW) in Washington DC, said creativity is a mental process by which an individual creates new ideas or products, or recombines existing ideas and products, in a fashion that is novel to him or to her (Gallagher, 1985). This definition is similar to that of R. Keith Sawyer (2006) in *Explaining Creativity: The Science of Innovation*, who defined creativity as the emergence of something novel and appropriate from a person, a group, or a society. Sawyer goes on to explain creativity as "big C" creativity and "little c" creativity. Big C creativity involves finding solutions to extremely difficult problems or significant works of genius, while little c includes activities people engage in every day, such as modifying a recipe when you don't have all the ingredients, avoiding a traffic jam by finding a new way through side streets, or figuring out how to apologize to a friend for an unintended insult. This definition of creativity is similar to that of psychologist Abraham Maslow (1970), who suggested there were two types of creativity, primary creativity and secondary creativity. Primary creativity involves great works of art and music, and secondary creativity could be a "fine soup."

Teresa Amabile, a parent of a gifted child and researcher in creativity, proposed a consensual definition of creativity. She said a product is creative when experts in the domain agree it is creative, and if experts from a domain come to consensus, it means that product is appropriate in that domain (Amabile, 1983).

Tracy Cross and Laurence Coleman, psychologists active in the field of gifted education, in *Being Gifted in School: An Introduction to Development, Guidance, and Teaching* offered a working definition of creativity. They said creativity is a general process expressed in many aspects of life and that creative expression becomes increasingly more specific with more experience and commitment to a variety of areas of knowledge and skill. The general process of creativity is transformed by fields of interest (Cross & Coleman, 2001). In other words, creativity becomes more field related as Amabile suggested, and the creative act can then be judged by criteria relevant to a field of inquiry.

CREATIVITY AS A COMPONENT OF GIFTEDNESS

The three-ring conception of giftedness was developed by Joseph Renzulli, a pioneer in gifted education in the early 1970s. He described the traditional view of the concept of giftedness as mainly a function of high scores on intelligence tests, and suggested that giftedness was made up of three rings—above average, but not necessarily superior ability; creativity; and task commitment—which he called the TRIAD model. Later, Renzulli embedded these three rings in a houndstooth background representing interactions between personality and environment. He said personality and environmental factors influence and aid in the development of the three clusters of traits that represent gifted behaviors (Renzulli, 1977).

This definition of giftedness is quite popular throughout the United States in that it de-emphasizes the use of IQ tests to identify giftedness and provides more opportunities for larger numbers of children to be considered for gifted programs. However, the major problem with this definition is not all intellectually gifted students are creative, nor are all creative students intellectually gifted. Yet, there appears to be a threshold intellectual ability level for creativity to develop.

CREATIVELY GIFTED AS A RECOGNIZED CATEGORY OF EXCEPTIONALITY

At the 1967 annual meeting of the National Association for Gifted Children (NAGC), E. Paul Torrance proposed "creatively gifted" be designated as a category in the field of special education or exceptional children. In the Marland (1972) report to Congress, creatively gifted was recognized as one of the categories of giftedness by the Office of Gifted and Talented. As a result, many state departments of education have approved the use of creativity tests as one instrument for identifying gifted children for programs supported by state funds.

Importance of Providing a "Fair Chance" to Creatively Gifted Students

In a paper presented at the 1968 institute on creativity convened by Calvin Taylor, another pioneer in creativity research and education, Toynbee said:

> To give a fair chance to creativity is a matter of life and death in any society. Creativity in a child can be discouraged easily and under hostile public opinion, the creative child is ready to purchase at almost any price the toleration that is an egalitarian-minded society's alluring reward for poor-spirited conformity. (p. 51)

Torrance stressed that one of the most important ways that teachers and parents can help creatively gifted students is by understanding and accepting their divergence—their sensitivity, their capacity to be disturbed, their tendency to become so involved and committed that they lose a sense of time, and their tendency to seek new and original solutions. He said humor is one of the favorite outlets of creatively gifted students and it can also become one of their weapons. Under restrictive and prescriptive teaching, misbehavior of various kinds, as well as humor, provide opportunities for creating excitement in an otherwise dull, monotonous, and despairing experience (Torrance, 1962a). An example of this type of behavior was noted when a group of Mount Union College students in Alliance, Ohio, completely dismantled a car and then reassembled it on the third floor of Chapman Hall.

Therefore, it is essential that school districts and parents strive to meet the unique needs of creative children, and because they are motivated to do the things that they do well, it is essential that schools provide opportunities for them to learn in creative ways, to solve problems in creative ways, and to live in a creative way. This can be realized if schools make a sincere effort to build a "creative consciousness."

Ways to Build Creative Consciousness

Fleith (2000) and Rejskind (2000) suggested a number of ways to build and demonstrate creative consciousness:

- Maintain a psychologically safe classroom environment.
- Help students become aware of their creativity.
- Recognize and reward each child's creativity.
- Encourage fantasy and imagination.
- Accept students as they are.
- Give positive constructive evaluation.
- Help students resist peer pressure to conform.
- Recognize students' strengths, abilities, and interests.
- Encourage questions, different responses, humor, and risk-taking.
- Be aware that a child's difficult behavior could be a manifestation of creativity.

THE INCUBATION MODEL ADDRESSES THE WHOLE OF CREATIVITY

Torrance developed the Incubation Model as a way of addressing the whole of creativity. He wanted to open the minds of students through creative activities and to keep those minds open to learning about a topic, even when a formal lesson was completed. The Incubation Model is made up of three stages: Stage 1 is called "Heightening Anticipation." Stage 2 involves motivating and encouraging the expected and unexpected, and it is called "Deepening Expectations." Stage 3 involves going beyond and is known as "Keeping It Going."

Stage 1 is made up of fifteen teaching strategies in which the teacher focuses on creating a desire to know, building heightened anticipation and expectation, getting attention, arousing curiosity, tickling the imagination, and providing purpose and motivation. Figure 8.1 depicts the Incubation Model. In this chapter, we will concentrate on Stage 1 of the Incubation Model—Heightening Anticipation—which consists of the fifteen strategies for teachers to use in nurturing and developing creativity in their students:

1. Confronting ambiguities and uncertainties.

2. Questioning to heighten expectation and anticipation.

3. Creating awareness of a problem to be solved, a possible future need, or a difficulty to be faced.

4. Building on the students' existing knowledge.

5. Heightening concern about a problem or future need.

6. Stimulating curiosity and the desire to know.

7. Making the strange familiar or the familiar strange.

8. Freeing from inhibiting mind-sets.

9. Looking at the same information from different viewpoints.

10. Provocative questioning to encourage thinking about information in new ways.

11. Predicting from limited information.

12. Making the purposefulness of the lesson clear, showing the connection between unexpected learning and present problems or future careers.

13. Providing only enough structure to give clues and direction.

14. Taking the next step beyond what is known.

15. Physically or bodily warming up as the information is presented.

Implementing the Incubation Model

One question often asked concerning the Incubation Model is whether it can be used with all grades. The answer is yes. For example, in the first class of a graduate course in education focusing on creativity in science, the teachers were posed Strategy 10, "Provocative questioning to encourage thinking about information in new ways." "What would happen if we had germs and viruses, or so-called super bugs, that had become resistant to antibiotics?" This strategy was paired with Strategy 6, "Stimulating curiosity and the desire to know," with the following information provided by their instructor: "Recently in Peru, scientists found a drug-resistant TB virus, and the research team posed the possibility of this drug-resistant

Figure 8.1　Incubation Model

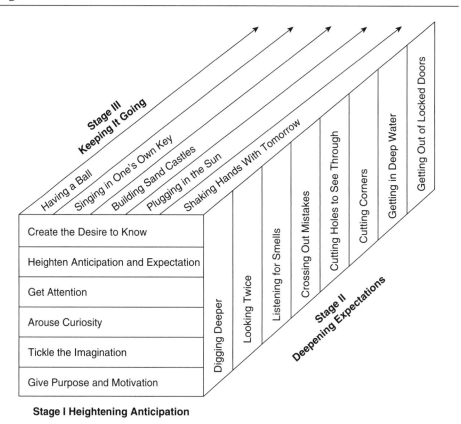

Source: From Sisk, D., & Torrance, E. P., (2001). *Spiritual intelligence: Developing higher consciousness.* Reprinted with permission of the Creative Education Foundation.

virus being passed on to others." Then the teachers were asked to focus on Strategy 14, "Taking the next step beyond what is known." The instructor said, "In this class we will have opportunities to research drug-resistant "super bugs" and the role of the World Health Organization."

There was free-flowing discussion in the class after this statement, and the instructor added the challenge of staph infections and their resistance to antibiotics. This information led to Strategy 6, "Stimulating curiosity and the desire to know," as two of the teachers shared viewing a PBS special on global health problems, and suggested the class secure a copy of this program. Another teacher demonstrated Strategy 4, "Building on the students' existing knowledge," by saying she had read about the work of Dr. Kim from Harvard, and how he and his colleagues were creating a new cocktail of drugs to fight drug-resistant "super bugs" in TB patients. At this point in the discussion, another teacher added that research was being conducted by scientists who were examining soil for possible particles that could naturally fight bacteria. Then the instructor suggested, "I would like each of you to formulate a research question with a focus on global health, and share your questions with one another. The teachers began writing their questions, and eight questions with similar emphases were identified and listed:

1. What is happening in India with the focus on immunization of children for smallpox?

2. What is happening with the TB breakout in Nigeria?

3. Why do some people have natural immunity to viruses?

4. Why isn't more being done to develop new antibiotics? Is it because there is little profit in this?

5. What are the side effects of taking cocktails of antibiotics?

6. Communicable diseases can travel anywhere in hours. What can be done about this or what is being done to combat this?

7. Can a strong public health infrastructure and proper nutrition protect people from infectious diseases?

8. Are there other "super bugs," such as SARS, Ebola virus, West Nile virus and Avian flu?

The twenty teachers selected questions from the eight that were listed, and natural groupings soon evolved to enable the search for information. All of this "teacher creativity" emerged in the first night of class using the Incubation Model. The enthusiasm of the group was captured in a comment of one of the teachers, "These questions get us involved in the real-life drama of creative scientists seeking solutions to these horrendous problems."

CASE STUDY

Mrs. Horton's first-second grade combination cluster group of gifted children is studying man's interaction with nature as an organizing theme in science. Prior to the beginning of the lesson, she noticed an article in the local paper about a proposed development in a coastal town and the possible danger to the natural habitat it posed. Mrs. Horton, a "dedicated environmentalist," decided to discuss the notion of "loss of habitat" with her children. She had been introduced to the Incubation Model of Torrance in a graduate class, and wanted to use it in planning her lesson. She used Strategy 3, "Creating awareness of a problem to be solved, a possible future need, or a difficulty to be faced"; Strategy 4, "Building on the students' existing knowledge"; and Strategy 9, "Looking at the same information from different viewpoints."

When the twenty students gathered together in their conversation center, Mrs. Horton said, "Today I am going to introduce a word to you that your older brothers and sisters are learning about in science." The children leaned forward in anticipation, and watched as

(Continued)

(Continued)

Mrs. Horton wrote the word on the flip chart. She said, "It is *habitat*; let's all say it together," and the children chorused "habitat." She continued, "Habitat is another word for home." The children focused on the teacher as she selected one of their favorite books, *Adventures of Peter Rabbit,* from the previous year's Pre-K cluster class. Mrs. Horton said, "Do you remember how Peter felt when he wanted to go home?" Several of the children replied: "He wanted his mother." "He was hungry." "He was scared." "He didn't like sleeping in the shed." Mrs. Horton smiled and responded, "Those are all great answers. Peter wanted to be at home with his mother, to get something to eat and to feel safe, and to sleep in his own bed. He wanted his habitat, or home." When we go outside today, let's see if we can find the habitat of some animals in our playground.

Mrs. Horton had skillfully summarized the responses of her students as they connected the word *habitat* to their knowledge of the story of Peter Rabbit. As they walked outside, Makela said, "My dog has a habitat: it's his doghouse." She grinned and ran off, very pleased with herself in sharing this piece of information with her teacher. As soon as Mrs. Horton went outside, she bent down noticing a lizard scurrying out of the way of the flying feet of the children. Several students stopped to see what she was observing, and she said, "This lizard has a habitat, a home here in our playground, and he's running to be safe." Cody added, "Look, Mrs. Horton there are ants over here, and one is carrying part of a cracker." Mrs. Horton drew near and said, "Be careful Cody, you don't want to get one of the ants on you; it will sting." Cody stepped back and replied, "I know I got ants on me at a picnic, and it hurt really bad."

Several of the children spotted a squirrel, and they watched as it ran up a tree and jumped to the roof of their school. Maeve said, "He has a habitat: the tree." Mrs. Horton knelt down and began to dig a small hole in the moist ground near their classroom, and then said, "Look, boys and girls, this worm has a habitat." Several of the children came forward to eagerly look at the worm that wriggled away from Mrs. Horton's fingers, burrowing deep in the dirt. Joshua said, "He's hiding. He likes the wet dirt." Mrs. Horton nodded and said, "He wants to be safe too." As the children moved around in their playground, which was located near a heavily wooded area, they noticed grasshoppers, dragonflies, beetles, and spiders. Also, birds were hopping in the grass searching for insects and "people food" from the last class. When Mrs. Horton called the students together to return to the classroom, she again assembled the class in their Conversation Center. She asked the children to share what they had noticed. She listed their responses on a flip chart in two columns: "I Notice" and "I Wonder," and she observed that several of the children were reading along with her. Because the class was a cluster class of gifted students, several of them were already successful readers.

Mrs. Horton said, "Have any of you visited the beach?" The children shared: "My family goes on Sunday when Dad goes fishing." "We go with my grandpa, and he takes a net to catch little fish for bait." "We went out on a boat and saw dolphins." "The pelicans fly over where we go—in a long line." Mrs. Horton smiled at their eagerness to share and said, "That is their home, their habitat. What would happen if someone built a huge hotel, and a golf course there?" The children thought for a while, and Tyler said, "They would need a new home—a habitat." He grinned happily at his use of the new word.

Mrs. Horton said, "Later on, we are going to use a simulation, and I will give each of you a card with a name on it, such as a dolphin, pelican, red fish, rabbit, mayor of a city, city council members who help the mayor, a contractor or developer who builds hotels, and citizens or people. Each of you will play a role like an actor, and we will discuss the proposal to build a new hotel." For example, "What might the pelicans say about building a big hotel where they fly and build nests?" Makela's hand shot up and she said, "I won't have a place to build my nest; they will cut down my trees." Mrs. Horton nodded and said, "We are going to have a visitor tomorrow who will talk to us about the coastal area habitat." She continued, "Mr. Jacobs is his name and he has written several books on the importance of learning about nature and taking care of the environment."

The students enthusiastically interacted with the visiting speaker, and he showed them many slides of different animals living in the coastal area, including an alligator that no one had mentioned, and Mrs. Horton agreed to add an alligator tag for one of the students to wear. Mr. Jacobs said he would like to come and observe their simulation.

The simulation was a huge success as the students wore their name tags of animals, the mayor, city council members, and citizens. Mrs. Horton asked Mr. Jacobs to role-play the builder, and the animal-players were seated in the front row as the simulation began. Mr. Jacobs said, "I plan to build a $80 million hotel with five stories, a pool, and a golf course." Tom, who was a dolphin, said, "How great!" Then he was nudged by Makela, a pelican, who said, "You won't use the pool, and they will have boats that could hurt you with their propellers." The children listened as Mr. Jacobs talked about the wonderful facilities, the five huge parking areas, and the many benefits to the citizens. However, the three citizen-players looked disturbed when they heard about the plans. "What about the animals? What do they say?" The animal-players said the pelicans would not fly over that area because of the people, and filling in part of the coastal area worried them. "Where would we live?" said the fish-player.

When it came time for them to vote, the teacher said "The mayor and the city council members can vote, and so can the citizens." But she quietly added, "The animals will not have a vote." At this point, the pelican, the dolphin, the fish, and the seagull shouted, "That's not fair. Who is going to vote for us?" Two of the citizens said, "We won't vote for the hotel." The third citizen said, "I'm going to vote for the hotel; it sounds wonderful." Mrs. Horton turned to the city council members and asked them to vote. It was a tie, with two council members voting for the hotel and two against. The mayor voted for the hotel, and Mrs. Jacobs was not surprised because Cody's father works as a manager in a hotel in their town.

Mrs. Horton thanked all of the players and began to discuss and debrief the simulation with the children using the following six questions:

1. What was the most difficult part in the role-playing for you?

2. Can something like building a big hotel be both a good thing and a bad thing?

3. How can we give a voice to the animals, if they don't have a vote?

4. How can we protect the habitat of the animals in the coastal area?

5. Did we have enough information to make a decision?

6. What else did we need to know?

The debriefing was one of the most exciting parts of the simulation, as the children pondered and reflected on the impact of building a large hotel in a coastal area that was a habitat for a great number of wildlife, and also a recreation area for local people and visitors. They all agreed they needed to know much more. Mrs. Horton noticed that the students who were the animal-players were receiving many kind words and even hugs from the other children. She said, "I hope we will always keep a loving and caring relationship with the animals in our environment."

By encouraging the students to use their higher-order thinking in the simulation, Mrs. Horton was able to motivate her students to use their creativity to ponder and reflect in a personalized and meaningful way on the importance of recognizing the interaction of people with their environment, and the need to become stewards of the environment.

BARRIERS TO THINKING CREATIVELY

There are three major barriers to thinking creatively.

1. Mind-sets (I'm not creative!)

2. Thought habits (thinking about the old ways)

3. Attitudes (daydreaming and wondering are a waste of time!)

It's amazing how many people say they aren't creative, and they usually add that a teacher or a parent told them they weren't creative; consequently, they didn't try to be creative. Thought habits that include focusing on the old ways of doing things can keep new ideas from emerging. However, the biggest deterrent to creative thinking is the idea that daydreaming and just wondering "What would happen if?" are a waste of time.

Ways of Breaking Barriers to Creative Thinking

The Creative Problem Solving Institute provides an annual conference to promote the five-step process originated by Alex Osborne and Sid Parnes to develop creative thinking. The creative problem solving process includes: fact-finding, problem-finding, idea-finding, solution-finding, and acceptance-finding. In fact-finding, participants list all of the known facts about a problem and gather as much data about the problem as possible. In problem-finding, the participants write or state the problem in a well-defined procedure by asking "In what ways might I?" In idea-finding, the emphasis is on generating as many ideas as possible, and brainstorming is used with no judgment placed on any of the ideas. The goal in this stage of the creative problem-solving process is to list as many ideas as possible, giving free rein to imagination. Solution-finding involves choosing the alternatives with the greatest potential for solving the problem, and the last step is acceptance-finding or developing a plan of action. The five step process is illustrated in Figure 8.2.

Figure 8.2   Five Step Creative Problem Solving Process

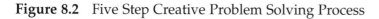

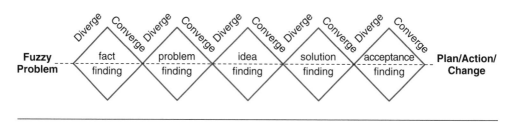

Young gifted students love brainstorming. They take to it naturally because they are free in generating ideas and haven't developed the strong sense of evaluation that older gifted students have. One way to encourage gifted students to increase their flow of ideas is to use the list of idea spurring questions of Alex Osborne (1963):

1. Put to other uses? New ways to use "as is"? Other uses if modified?

2. Adapt? What else is like this? What other ideas does this suggest?

3. Modify? Change meaning, color, motion, sound, odor, taste, form, shape? Other changes?

4. Magnify? What to add? Greater frequency? Stronger? Larger?

5. Minify? What to subtract? Eliminate? Smaller? Lighter? Slower? Split up?

6. Substitute? Who else instead? What else instead? Other place? Other time?

7. Rearrange? Other layout? Other sequences? Change pace?

8. Reverse? Opposite? Turn it backwards?

9. Combine? How about a blend? Combine ideas?

Doris Shallcross (1981), author of *Teaching Creative Behavior*, suggested that teachers use seven questions to encourage gifted students to move to the implementation stage in creative problem solving by taking action and drawing up a plan. Her ideas call for the students to engage in a dialogue with themselves. They can ask: What has to happen before anything else can happen? Who else will be involved? Does someone have to be convinced this is a good idea? What strategy can I use for convincing others? What materials are needed? Do we need to rearrange our schedules? And, does anything need to be sacrificed to put these ideas into action?

MEASURING CREATIVITY

The initial impetus for the development of measures of creativity included the work of J. P. Guilford (1959) and E. P. Torrance (1962b). Guilford viewed creativity as an essential component of intellectual functioning, and included it as a part of the Structure of Intellect Model as divergent thinking. He identified the factors of creativity as fluency, flexibility, originality, and elaboration. These factors became the categories of creative thinking in the measures of creativity developed by Torrance in the late 1960s and early 1970s.

Creativity as Process

The Torrance Test of Creative Thinking (TTCT-1074) measures creativity as a process and operationalizes creativity as a divergent production including fluency, flexibility, originality, and elaboration. Later, Torrance added several more dimensions to the figural tests. The TTCT requires students to demonstrate their fluency by giving large numbers of answers to a question; their flexibility in giving a variety of responses; their originality in providing unique, but relevant answers; and their elaboration in taking an existing idea or product and modifying or changing it. Figure 8.3 depicts an item called *Product Improvement*. The students are shown a picture of a ship and asked to make it more fun to play with by changing the ship in "interesting, clever, and unusual ways" The students might change the ship's shape, color, size, position, and so on. They might add that the ship could talk, squirt water, or fly. They could add an engine or a horn. The total number of answers the student gives measures fluency, the different kinds of answers measures flexibility, and the uniqueness of the answers measures originality.

Figure 8.3   Product Improvement Item Adapted from the TTCT

Figure of ship

Source: Product Improvement—Torrance, E. P. (1962). *Thinking creatively with words.* Bensenville, IL: Scholastic Testing Service, Inc.

The Torrance tests are available in four test booklets—Forms A and B for each of the two tests: "Thinking Creatively with Words" (verbal) and "Thinking Creatively with Pictures" (nonverbal, figural) (Torrance, 1974). The verbal battery includes six subtests that require students to ask questions and to list unusual uses for objects, improvements for toys, and consequences of an unlikely event. The figural battery includes three subsets, involving an incomplete or abstract sketch that students need to transform into a meaningful picture.

Creativity Using Person Perspective

Measures that identify the creative student using the person perspective include inventory measures of characteristics. This type of measurement requires the observation or self-report of personal characteristics or attitudes in inventories such as the "Alpha Biographical Inventory" (Taylor & Ellison, 1967) and the "Group Inventory for Finding Interests" (GIFT) (Rimm & Davis, 1976). In these inventories, the students identify themselves by agreeing with personality descriptions highly linked to creative behavior such as:

I am very curious.

I am a risk taker.

I am witty.

I have engaged in a lot of creative activities.

Other inventories include Schaefer's (1970) "Creativity Attitude Survey" and Williams's (1980) "Exercise in Divergent Thinking" that can be used with elementary students. Khatena & Torrance (1976) developed an inventory called "Something About Myself" and "What Kind of Person Are You?" that can be used with adolescents and adults.

Identifying creative students can also be accomplished through informal observations and interviews. For example, does the student display creative personality and motivational characteristics? Does the student have a background of creative activities? In high school, a background in theater can indicate creative potential. Imaginary playmates are another aspect of creativity that can be noted in interviews, and these imaginary playmates are noted with both children and adults. Renzulli (1983) developed a checklist of creativity characteristics that is used in many schools to identify students with creative potential. Some of the items on this checklist include the following:

1. Displays a keen sense of humor and sees humor in situations that may not seem humorous to others

2. Is sensitive to beauty, attends to aesthetic characteristics of things

3. Is a high risk-taker, adventurous, and speculative

ARE YOU CREATIVE?

Numerous lists of creative characteristics are available, but Davis (1995) did what he called an "eyeball factor analysis" and generated a list of twelve characteristics. These are listed with questions for you to use to reflect on the personality characteristics of creative people. Read the following list and see if you think you are creative.

1. *Aware of creativeness-creativity conscious.* Do you value your own creativity?

2. *Original.* Do you see yourself as resourceful and nonconforming?

3. *Independent.* Are you self-confident and unconcerned with impressing others?

4. *Risk-taking.* Are you optimistic and unconcerned with impressing others?

5. *Energetic.* Are you spontaneous and impulsive?

6. *Curious.* Are you open to new experiences and growth?

7. *Sense of humor.* Are you playful and fresh in your thinking?

8. *Attracted to complexity.* Are you attracted to novelty and tolerant of ambiguity?

9. *Artistic.* Are you artistic and aesthetic?

10. *Open-minded.* Are you receptive to new ideas?

11. *Needs time alone.* Are you introspective and like to work by yourself?

12. *Intuitive.* Are you perceptive, see relationships and use all of your senses? (pp. 70–71)

IMPORTANCE OF CREATIVITY IN YOUR LIFE

Most people express their creativity in their daily lives in simple tasks, and it is important to remember that Maslow thought making a good soup was creative, if you use your "very own recipe." In addition, there is creativity in performance, and many gifted students participate in musical and theater performances, expressing their creativity in portraying a role in drama or in performing a piece of music. But most important, creativity is fun. The participants in the Creative Problem Solving Institute describe their experiences as positive and self-actualizing, but almost all of them add that it was "fun."

One important caveat to remember in the development of creativity is to select a domain or field that is right for you and focus on that one area. When you find an area that you love, your intrinsic motivation will carry you through. You must believe in yourself and be willing to take risks. Donald MacKinnon (1987), a well-known researcher in creativity, found in his studies that creative people were happy and successful, and they had well-balanced personalities. The importance of achieving balance in your life is explored in Chapter 9.

SUMMARY

This chapter examined the definitions of creativity and explored the theory that creativity is a part of giftedness, as posed by Joseph Renzulli in the TRIAD model. The chapter examined a second theory of conceptualizing creativity as a unique type of giftedness, as posed by E. Paul Torrance. The importance of providing a fair chance to creatively gifted students was discussed, and ways to build creative consciousness using the Torrance Incubation Model, which addresses the whole of creativity, was presented. Examples of implementing the Incubation Model in teacher education and in a case study of a first and second grade combination cluster group of gifted students were provided. Barriers to creativity were identified, along with ways of breaking those barriers, such as using creative problem solving as developed by Alex Osborne and Sid Parnes. Measures of creativity as a process using the Torrance Test of Creative Thinking were discussed, as well as observation instruments and inventories for measuring creativity from the person perspective. The importance of creativity in one's life was stressed, and a checklist for assessing individual creativity called *Are You Creative?* based on categories developed by Gary Davis, was provided.

Teacher Voice

After reading this chapter on developing creativity in gifted students, several thoughts came to mind. First, I agree that creativity can be developed—especially through problem solving. Second, I believe that creativity in our students is being stifled, first through our current life style and second at school. Students do not spend time outdoors looking, observing, building, and using their imagination for play. Teachers need to build in the time to allow students to explore and to become curious, as this leads to designing ways to learn more. Another way that teachers can increase creativity in the classroom is by allowing students to build models, draw diagrams, and develop their own assessments. Many times, if several options are available as suggested in the chapter, the teacher will see a wide variety of creative products. I had one student—he didn't like to complete any written assignment. We had a project in which they were going to design the DNA of a creature and then build a model and write a story. Johnny wanted his to breathe real fire. I truly didn't think he would be able to do so, so I said, "Sure, why not?" Two weeks later, he brought his creature rolling into the classroom, and after getting all the safety equipment, we had a fire breathing creature in the classroom. The other students thought it was super. Any time Johnny had a hands-on project where he could be creative, he did a great job.

Susan Ellis
Middle school teacher

Read On

Cupertino, C. (2007). Differentiating curriculum for gifted students through creative workshops. *Gifted International*, *23*(1), 19–31.

Davis, G. (1992). *Creativity is forever*. Dubuque, IA: Kendall-Hunt.

Fowler, S., Yates, T., & Lewman, B. (2007). Using a weekly story to plan creative activities and promote early literacy in preschool. *GCT*, *30*(3), 27–39.

Sternberg, R. (2000). Creating a vision of creativity: The first 25 years. *Psychology of Aesthetic, Creativity and the Arts*, *8*(12), 2–12.

Zhao, Y. (2006). Are we fixing the wrong things? *Educational Leadership*, *63*(8), 28–31.

Log On

Association for Experiential Education (http://www.aee.org/). Provides resources to make direct, hands-on experience central in teaching.

Edutopia Online (http://www.edutopia.org/projectbasedlearning/). A Web site created by the George Lucas Educational Foundation, with the information and resources for implementing project-based learning.

The National Association for Secondary School Principals (http://www.nassp.org/). Includes a list of contests and creative activities.

Seussville (http://www.seussville.com/). A Web site for Seuss fans. You can create your own story with the Seussville Story Maker or enjoy some of the best Seuss quotes with the Quote Maker. Also provides the biography of Dr. Seuss.

Reflect On

- Creativity and not standardization may be the driving force behind an effective education system. What do you think? Is No Child Left Behind the culprit?
- Bertrand Russell once said, "In all affairs it's a healthy thing now and then to hang a question mark on the things you have long taken for granted." What could you do in a different way to bring creativity in your life or in your classroom?
- Helen Keller said life is either a daring adventure or nothing. What do you think? Can you add a daring adventure to your life?

- Joseph Campbell in *The Power of Myth* (Campbell & Moyer, 1988) said if you follow your bliss, you put yourself on a kind of track that has been there all the while, waiting for you, and the life that you ought to be living is the one that you are living. What do you think he was saying about finding your true talent, your true goal, your true purpose?

REFERENCES

Amabile, T. (1983). *The social psychology of creativity*. New York: Springer-Verlag.

Campbell, J., & Moyer, B. (1988). *The power of myth*. New York: Doubleday.

Cross, T., & Coleman, L. (2001). *Being gifted in school: An introduction to development, guidance, and teaching*. Waco, TX: Prufrock Press.

Cupertino, C. (2007). Differentiating curriculum for gifted students through creative workshops. *Gifted International, 23*(1), 19–31.

Davis, G. (1992). *Creativity is forever*. Dubuque, IA: Kendall-Hunt.

Davis, G. (1995). Identifying the creatively gifted. In J. Genshaft, M. Bireley, & M. Hollinger (Eds.), *Serving gifted and talented students: A research guide for school personnel*. Austin, TX: Pro-ed.

Davis, G. (2003). Identifying creative students. In N. Colangelo & G. Davis (Eds.), *Handbook of gifted education* (pp. 311–324). New York: Pearson Education.

Fleith, D. (2000). Teachers and students' perception of creativity in the classroom. *Roeper Review, 22*, 148–157.

Fowler, S., Yates, T., & Lewman, B. (2007). Using a weekly story to plan creative activities and promote early literacy in preschool. *GCT, 30*(3), 27–39.

Gallagher, J. (1985). *Teaching the gifted child*. Boston: Allyn & Bacon.

Guilford, J. P. (1959). Three faces of intellect. *American Psychologist, 14*, 469–479.

Khatena, J., & Torrance, E. P. (1976). *Manual for Khatena-Torrance creative perceptions inventory*. Chicago: Stoeling.

MacKinnon, D. (1987). Some critical issues for future research in creativity. In S. G. Isaksen (Ed.), *Frontiers of creativity research* (pp. 120–130). Buffalo, NY: Bearly.

Marland, S. (1972). *Education of the gifted and talented*. Report to the Congress of the United States by the U.S. Commissioner of Education. Washington, DC: U.S. Government Printing Office.

Maslow, A. (1970). *Motivation and personality*. New York: Harper & Row.

Osborne, A. (1963). *Applied imagination*. New York: Charles Limited.

Parnes, S. J. (1981). *The magic of your mind*. Buffalo, NY: Bearly.

Piechowski, M. (2006). *Mellow out they say, if only I could: Intensities and sensitivities of the young and bright*. Madison, WI: Yunasa Books.

Pierce, J. (1998). Purposeful creativity: The six P's of creative problem solving. In R. Crandall (Ed.), *Creativity breakthrough* (pp. 35–50). Corte Madera, CA: Select Press.

Rejskind, G. (2000). TAG teachers: Only the creative need apply. *Roeper Review, 22*, 153–157.

Renzulli, J. (1977). *The enrichment TRIAD model: A guide for developing defensible programs for the gifted and talented*. Wethersfield, CT: Creative Learning Press.

Renzulli, J. (1983). Rating behavioral characteristics of superior students. *GCT, 15*, 30–35.

Rimm, S., & Davis, G. (1976). GIFT: An instrument for the identification of creativity. *Journal of Creative Behavior, 10*, 178–182.

Sawyer, R. (2006). *Explaining creativity: The science of innovation*. New York: Oxford University Press.

Schaefer, C. E. (1970). *Biographical inventory—Creativity*. San Diego, CA: Educational and Industrial Testing Services.

Shallcross, D. (1981). *Teaching creative behavior*. Englewood Cliffs, NJ: Prentice Hall.

Sisk, D., & Torrance, E. P. (2001). *Spiritual intelligence: Developing higher consciousness*. New York: Creative Education Foundation.

Sternberg, R. (2000). Creating a vision of creativity: The first 25 years. *Psychology of Aesthetic, Creativity and the Arts, 8*(12), 2–12.

Taylor, C. W., & Ellison, R. L. (1967). Biographical predictors of scientific performance. *Science, 155,* 1075–1080.

Torrance, E. P. (1962a). *Guiding creative talent.* Englewood Cliffs, NJ: Prentice Hall.

Torrance, E. P. (1962b). *Thinking creatively with words.* Bensenville, IL: Scholastic Test Service.

Torrance, E. P. (1974). *Torrance tests of creative thinking: Norms-technical manual.* Lexington, MA: Personnel Press.

Toynbee, A. (1968). Is America neglecting her creative talents? In C. Taylor (Ed.), *Creativity across education.* Ogden: University of Utah Press.

Williams, F. (1980). *Creativity assessment packet.* Buffalo, NY: DOK.

Zhao, Y. (2006). Are we fixing the wrong things? *Educational Leadership, 63*(8), 28–31.

9

Developing a Sense of Peace and Tranquility

Gifted students with their sensitivity and empathy for others are deeply troubled by the conflict and uncertainty in today's world. They are bombarded daily with scenes of violence, racial injustice, sexual abuse, alcoholism, environmental exploitation, and many other problems in the evening news, in movies, and in video games, and they can easily become overwhelmed. The danger for gifted children and for society is that people may come to accept violence as a way of life. However, giftedness creates a different worldview in which impossible dreams can be realized, unrealistic goals achieved, insurmountable obstacles surmounted by individuals whose vision represents a more powerful reality than the limitations most of the world accept as "real" (Silverman, 1998).

In this chapter, we explore the importance of the concept that peace begins with the individual. Ways that a sense of peace and tranquility can be introduced to gifted children, as suggested by Thich Nhat Hanh (2005), such as simply sitting on the grass with a young child and pointing out the tiny yellow and blue flowers that grow among the grasses, and contemplating these miracles together, are discussed. We address the question: How can we hold strong differences of view in a larger context of unity beyond discord and hostility? This focus leads to examples of practical applications for developing a sense of peace and tranquility through meditation to enable great kids to become greater and ease the burden of being gifted. A case study of a gifted high school student using mindfulness to plan and to develop a Loving Hands Project in her high school, in her university, and eventually in her lifework, is presented. Examples of universities providing peace education are identified, and the Seeds of Peace program is explored as a concerted effort to build peace with teenagers from war-torn countries. A section on negotiation and conflict resolution as essential skills for seeking peace and managing conflicts constructively is introduced as a life skill for gifted students.

REACHING ONE'S IDEAL SELF

The drive for reaching one's ideal self manifests in a dissatisfaction with "what is" and a yearning to become what one "ought to be" (Dabrowski & Piechowski, 1977). The challenge for gifted kids is to develop the ability to tap their inner knowing to sense that there is so much more available in life, and to use their inner knowing to achieve a sense of peace and tranquility.

A Heart Full of Peace

The Sanskrit word *maitri* and the Pali word *metta* both mean "loving kindness" or loving care, and refer to an attitude of friendliness, good will, and generosity of heart. Joseph Goldstein (2007) said the challenge is how to embody a heart full of peace in times of uncertainty and conflict. *Metta* is a caring and kindness that does not seek self-benefit and makes no distinction among people. Loving kindness embraces everyone, and no one falls outside of its domain. Examples of individuals who have developed the capacity of loving kindness include the Dalai Lama and Mother Teresa. These individuals would be classified as Level V in the Dabrowski multi-levels, or as people who assume responsibility for others, as well as responsibility for their own development. They are exemplars of empathy, compassion, and love turned into action.

Practicing Loving Kindness for Oneself

Goldstein, cofounder of Insight Meditation Society in Barre, Massachusetts, conducts seminars and retreats for educators, corporations, law firms, and individuals or groups that want to learn more about the experience of insight and self-development. He suggested the following activity as an introduction to practicing loving kindness:

> Sit in a comfortable chair or position, and keep an image of a felt sense of yourself in mind (you might want to visualize a miniature

you, with your hair color, clothes and facial features), and then slowly repeat the following phrases of loving kindness for yourself:

> *May I be happy.*
>
> *May I be peaceful.*
>
> *May I be free of suffering.*

(Goldstein, 2007, p. 6)

Goldstein suggested repeating these phrases that reflect feelings of care and well-wishing, and he makes a distinction between this practice and affirmations, in that the loving kindness practice is a caring *intention*. As you repeat the words, and focus your mind on the intention of kindness, it will slowly grow into a powerful force in your life.

An Example of a Loving Kindness Practice

A second grade teacher of a very diverse class, including Hispanic, Asian, African-American, and Anglo children, begins her day with the students repeating the following loving kindness statements:

> *May I be happy.*
>
> *May I be kind.*
>
> *May I be loving.*
>
> *May I be helpful.*

She said that her second grade students were praised for their behavior in the cafeteria and in the halls, "They don't push and shove, or shout at one another." In addition, she said the children approach their day of studies with a positive and expectant attitude when they begin their day with her version of a loving kindness practice.

The Practice of Loving Kindness for All

Goldstein suggested that loving kindness statements be made to people who have helped you, to loved ones, to those you have neutral feelings for, people for whom you have no strong feelings one way or another, and then to difficult people or enemies. Then, he recommended sending loving messages to people everywhere. Goldstein emphasized that in these practices, it is important to take time to visualize the individuals, and to generate genuine feelings of love for them. You can practice loving statements alone in your home, in your car, or even as you walk down the hall of your school or the street. In all cases, Goldstein said practicing loving kindness can change the way you relate to the world.

The nightly news programs are virtual catalogs of the world's distress, and you can become immune to what is heard or seen as the disasters become depersonalized. "It doesn't affect me." Consequently, it is important that we keep our minds open to the suffering of all the people in the world. If we want our lives to benefit everyone (Level V of Dabrowski), we need to develop a genuine empathy for others in pain or difficulty. Taking a moment to stop and to feel what's really going on, before rushing on with your life, moves you from empathy, a sympathetic feeling for others, to compassion—which is much more than warm feelings (Goldstein, 2007).

Great exemplars of compassion and social justice include people like Martin Luther King, Jr., Mohandas Gandhi, and Aung San Suu Ky. Gifted students can benefit from studying their lives, particularly having opportunities to listen to their speeches and to feel the emotion in their beliefs. Such studies can stimulate a "seed" for making positive change in themselves and in others. Thich Nhat Hanh, a Zen master, poet, and peace advocate, lives in a retreat called Plum Village in France, and he said many people are not really alive, because they are unable to touch life in the present moment. He suggested practicing conscious breathing, and as you breathe in, know that you are breathing in, and as you breathe out, know that you are breathing out. He suggested the following exercise (Hanh, 1992, pp. 11–12):

Breathing in, I see myself as a flower.

Breathing out, I feel fresh.

Flower/Fresh

Breathing in, I see myself as a mountain.

Breathing out, I feel solid.

Mountain/Solid

Breathing in, I see myself as water.

Breathing out, I reflect things as they are.

Water/Reflecting

Breathing in, I see myself as space.

Breathing out, I feel free.

Space/Free.

Hanh said the process of just breathing in and out can calm the storm of worries, anxieties, agitation, and sadness, so that you can find peace. Breathe in and say "flower," and breathe out and say "fresh." Use this same procedure for mountain/solid, water/reflecting, and space/free. These exercises are soothing, and Hanh said, "Breathing in and out consciously helps you become your best—calm, fresh, solid, clear, and free, able to enjoy the present moment as the best moment of your life" (p. 21). He recommended that we celebrate a day when we can live happily in the present moment throughout the day. He suggested it be called "Today's Day," a day dedicated to touching the earth, touching the sky, touching the trees, and touching the peace that is available in the present moment.

An Example of Loving Kindness for All

The idea of having a Today's Day was introduced to thirty-eight first grade students during a summer enrichment program when their teacher said, "We celebrate Mother's Day, Father's Day, Christmas, and Valentine's Day; why not Today's Day when we could celebrate the day by touching the earth?" The children thought it was a great idea. They ran about the playground touching trees, flowers, bushes, grass, and even reaching toward the sky, as if touching the clouds and sky. It was such a successful activity, the teacher decided to include Today's Day in all of her future classes. She thanked the children for sharing what they had touched and said, "We are celebrating life in the present moment, right *now*." The students were quite responsive to her enthusiasm, and in later years they will realize the full impact of celebrating Today's Day as they revisit their memories of living in the present moment.

MINDFULNESS

Mindfulness is the seed of enlightenment, awareness, understanding, care, compassion, liberation, transformation, and healing (Hanh, 1992). He said mindfulness makes life more beautiful, and if we touch the trees or flowers with mindfulness, we can begin to experience oneness with nature. In Plum Village, under the leadership of Thich Nhat Hanh, they practice a ceremony that includes an activity called Flower Watering. In this activity, when one person is ready to speak, she joins her palms, and the others join their palms to show that she has the right to speak. Then she stands, walks slowly to take a flower from a vase in the center of the room, and returns to her seat. When she speaks, her words reflect the freshness and beauty of the flower she holds. During Flower Watering, each speaker talks about the wholesome and wonderful qualities of the others. Hanh said it is not flattery, it is truth, and the speaker is allowed as much time as needed to speak. Everyone else practices *deep listening* or total focusing on the speaker. This activity is similar to a group dynamics activity in which one person is asked to take a center chair, and the group bombards him or her with positive statements. However, in Flower Watering, the speaker makes positive comments about others, and the focus is on positive affirmation to build a sense of community.

Guidelines for a Mindful Society

Thich Nhat Hanh (1992) in *Touching Peace: Practicing the Art of Mindful Living* proposed a set of guidelines for a mindful society. These guidelines can be used to introduce a peace education focus in social studies, in a summer enrichment program, or in service projects. Three of the five mindfulness training activities are included with suggestions on how to use them in peace education.

The First Mindfulness Training

> Aware of the suffering caused by the destruction of life, I am committed to cultivating compassion and learning ways to protect the lives of people, animals, plants, and minerals. I am determined not to kill, not to let others kill, and not to support any act of killing in the world, in my thinking, and in my way of life. (Hanh, 1992, p. 82)

This mindfulness training is committed to protecting the planet and to energizing individuals to love and compassion. It reflects a determination not to kill, either directly or indirectly, and to prevent others from killing. With *mindfulness*, you can see that lives everywhere are being destroyed, as well as the necessity of being committed to cultivating compassion for the protection of people, animals, plants, and the entire planet. Using this mindfulness training will help you to further develop an understanding of the destruction of life so you can decide what kind of action to take, which would include building an awareness of becoming stewards of the earth.

The Second Mindfulness Training

> Aware of the suffering caused by exploitation, social injustice, stealing, and oppression, I am committed to cultivating loving kindness and learning ways to work for the well-being of people, animals, plants, and minerals. I will practice generosity by sharing my time, energy, materials, and resources with those who are in real need. I am determined not to steal and not to possess anything that should belong to others. I will respect the property of others, but I will prevent others from profiting from human suffering or the suffering of other species on Earth. (Hanh, 1992, p. 83)

Hanh said stealing comes in many forms, including oppression that causes suffering, particularly in the third world where countries are torn by poverty. This second mindfulness training is about building awareness of suffering and cultivating loving kindness. It stresses that time is more valuable than money and that time can bring joy and happiness to other people and to ourselves. Hanh identified three gifts: (1) the gift of material resources, (2) the gift of helping people rely on themselves, and (3) the gift of non-fear. He stressed that helping people not be destroyed by fear is the greatest gift of all.

The Third Mindfulness Training

> Aware of the suffering caused by unmindful speech and the inability to listen to others, I am committed to cultivating loving speech, and deep listening in order to bring joy and happiness to others and relieve others of their suffering. I am determined to speak truthfully, with words that inspire self-confidence, joy and hope. I will not spread news that I do not know to be certain and will not criticize or condemn things of which I am not sure. I will refrain from uttering words that can cause division or discord, or that can cause the family or the community to break. I am determined to make all efforts to reconcile and resolve all conflicts, however small. (Hanh, 1992, p. 84)

Loving speech is an act of generosity, and when parents, teachers, and counselors use words that inspire confidence in gifted students, they will flourish and reach their potential. It is important to practice deep listening in this third mindfulness training. Deep listening is listening without prejudice and listening with total attention. Deep listening involves listening to what is being said, as well as what is not being said. A great deal of pain and suffering can be alleviated in another person simply by giving him or her your full attention and acceptance.

Goldstein (2007) said, when we are filled with loving kindness and a sense of loving care, we will have one simple wish: May all beings be happy. He stressed in situations of conflict, loving kindness and compassion will grow when we understand that they represent the most beneficial motivation for responsive and affective action. Goldstein said when we practice loving kindness and come close to the suffering in the world, we will be motivated to seek ways to alleviate it.

INSTINCT FOR COMPASSION

Darwin (1998) said that empathy was the prelude for compassionate action and a powerful aid for survival. Yet, paradoxically when a group of Princeton Theological Seminary students were involved in a study to measure their compassion and altruism, Goleman (2006) reported that most of them failed. Forty students were told to prepare short practice sermons, and one half of the students were assigned to use random biblical topics and the other half were assigned to use the parable of the Good Samaritan. The students worked together for about 15 minutes, then they were instructed to go to another building to present their practice sermons. The students did not know they were taking part in an experiment. To reach their assigned place for the practice sermons, they had to pass by an individual slumped in the doorway, groaning in pain. Twenty-four of the students passed by and ignored the man. There was no difference in the behavior of students assigned the Good Samaritan parable and the behavior of students assigned the random biblical topics. Ten of the students were told to hurry, as they thought they were going to be late. Of that group, only one stopped to help. Only six of the group who thought they had plenty of time offered help. The experiment indicated that when you are in a self-absorbed state, it is difficult to focus on someone in need.

In contrast to the behavior of the students, Goleman (2006) reported an experiment with rhesus monkeys in which six of them were trained to pull chains for food. The seventh monkey, in full view of the others, received a painful shock whenever one of the monkeys pulled a chain for food. Four of the monkeys pulled different chains that released less food but no shock. The fifth monkey stopped pulling any chain for five days, and the sixth monkey stopped pulling any chains for twelve days. Consequently, both monkeys were starving themselves to prevent shocking the seventh monkey. Goleman (2006) said this experiment illustrated an automatic impulse that focused their attention on another's suffering and triggered distressed feelings that led them to try and help. The difference in behavior between the students and the monkeys appeared to be the degree of self-absorption. When we are centered on ourselves, we respond to our own needs, in contrast to being other-centered, as described in Levels IV–V of the Dabrowski Theory of Emotional Development, in which one assumes responsibility for others as well as one's own development, and empathy and love are turned into action (Miller, 2006).

CONSCIOUSNESS METAPHOR

Thich Nhat Hanh (1992) said consciousness is divided into two parts, and he compared it to a house with two floors. On the ground floor is a living room, which he called the *mind consciousness.* Below the ground level there is a basement, which he called the *store consciousness.* In store consciousness, everything you have ever done, experienced, or perceived is stored in the form of a film. The basement is an archive of every imaginable kind of film stored on a videocassette. Upstairs in the living room, you sit in a chair and watch these films as they are brought up from the basement. This metaphor illustrates how we spend a great deal of time watching the same films over and over, and the importance of learning how to stop them. Hanh suggested focusing on what is beautiful and wholesome to aid in the transformation of thoughts, and to use meditation to quiet the mind and achieve tranquility.

MEDITATION

Meditation is an internal process of discovering and becoming familiar with your mind. By practicing meditation, you can develop insight into yourself, your motions, thoughts, and feelings. Meditation can help mindfulness to grow and to develop. You need to resolve to meditate regularly, such as several times a week, but for no longer than ten to fifteen minutes per session in the beginning. It is important to have expectations, but it is also necessary to realize that expecting too much at first can close you to the experience. Gill Farrer-Halls (2000) a writer, editor, and video producer who has worked closely with the Dalai Lama, identified three meditations that can help bring a sense of peace and tranquility: (1) tranquil abiding meditation, or letting go of thoughts; (2) insight meditation; and (3) walking meditation.

Tranquil Abiding: Letting Go of Thoughts

When you first begin to meditate, you may find you are dwelling on painful thoughts or memories, or on past positive experiences, and it is important to think of these as *impermanent* and concentrate on the meditation. Farrer-Halls (2000) said that when you decide to meditate, find a place that is quiet and available to you on a regular basis. She suggested getting up fifteen minutes early to meditate, or at night before bedtime. However, if you are too tired, you may fall asleep. During meditation, *correct posture* is important because the mind and body support each other. Incline your head slightly and loosely close your eyes or keep them partly open and look down. This helps to prevent distractions. Gently fold your arms, and rest your hands in your lap, with your palms upward. Relax your whole posture and feel free from tension. This helps your mind to become clear and calm. As you sit quietly in this position, be aware of being in the present, the here and now, and relax into this space. Try to let go of all of your thoughts, concerns about the future, nostalgia about the past, or worrying about problems. Maintain a balance between trying too hard and becoming drowsy. Bring your attention to your breathing and notice the sensation of breathing in and breathing out to help clear your mind. You may want to slowly count your breaths up to ten, and if your mind strays from the counting, gently, call it back. Your mind will wander, and it is important to not be too critical of yourself when you first begin to meditate. This first stage of meditation is known as *tranquil abiding* or *letting go of thoughts* (Farrer-Halls, 2000).

Insight Meditation

In insight meditation, the mind is used to inquire deeply into any phenomena that may arise in your mind. This means looking deeply at feelings and thoughts, and analyzing them. Again, it is important to sit quietly and calm your mind with deep breathing, and then observe your thoughts and feelings as they arise and pass. Bring your attention to whatever arises and focus on it. Deepen your focus by breathing in and out, and begin to analyze your thoughts and feelings. If you become distracted or upset, bring your focus back to your breathing. Spend a few minutes on mindfulness meditation, breathing in, and breathing out, and your mind will calm. Alternating between mindfulness meditation and insight meditation is helpful because the two meditation practices reinforce one another. Germer (2007), a clinical psychologist specializing in mindfulness training, said mindfulness practice involves both awareness and acceptance of present experience.

Walking Meditation

In walking meditation, the walking becomes the objective. Say to yourself, I'm not going anywhere, I am just walking. In walking meditation, you usually walk in a straight line for twenty feet, stop and then come back. Be conscious of each foot as you lift and put it down, and it is helpful to do this in time with your breathing. Alternating a walking meditation with a sitting meditation will enhance your awareness. Mindfulness is concerned with becoming aware of the *process* of your thinking, as well as your thoughts. A useful technique is to focus on a thought, perhaps an unpleasant thought and label it "pain" and let it go. If this thought returns, you can continue to label it and let it go, and eventually you can gain control of your mind. This is important for gifted students who often say, "I can't turn off my mind." By examining thought patterns that arise and pass, you can change them. Practicing mindfulness is training the mind to live in the present and not to dwell on the past.

Once you have mastered the concentration on your breathing and clearing your mind, then you can practice meditation anywhere: in the bath, on planes, and of course when you are walking, which provides the added pleasure of being out in nature.

MEDITATION FOR CHILDREN

Deborah Rozman (1988) in *Meditating With Children: The Art of Concentration and Centering* takes the meditation process into the elementary class in a creative way by using visualization skills. She founded Evergreen School, and her teachers are available to travel to other school districts to help teachers learn to use meditation with their students. Rozman listed the following results of groups that have used her ideas:

1. A calm vibration throughout the group

2. More receptivity on the part of the children

3. A sense of fellowship or community experience

4. An awakening sensitivity and empathy with other people

5. Deeper sharing

6. Acceptance of feelings

7. Increased creative expression

8. An improved self-concept

9. An awakening of the imagination and parts of themselves the children had not explored (p. 147)

Rozman deliberately decided to use the word *meditating* in the title of her book, in spite of knowing that some educators and parents would react negatively to the word and associate it with religion. She stressed the importance of restoring the term *meditation* to its rightful nonreligious definition, since meditation is based on a rich ancient tradition of confronting the mind and self to gain awareness. One of her meditations is called *spaceship meditation,* in which she suggested the teacher say:

> Imagine there is a spaceship inside of your head, step inside your spaceship. Now, go all the way up in your spaceship, out of the top of your head. Past billions of stars, up, up, up . . . (pause) . . . observe what you see, now go all the way down in your space ship . . . down, down, down . . . (pause) . . . now go all the way left . . . farther . . . now all the way straight in front of you, farther, farther, farther, farther . . . (pause) . . . now all the way behind go farther and farther back, on and on, farther and farther . . . (long pause). Now, come back slowly to the center and back into the top of your head and now you are inside your head again. You have traveled over and through the entire universe. Open your eyes, look around you. What did you see in your universe? Discuss with each other. (Rozman, 1988, p. 78)

In this delightful experience, the students use their creative imagery, and Rozman said she can plant seeds within them to awaken new realizations about life.

CASE STUDY

Allie attended a three-week residential leadership program with 150 gifted rising juniors in high school, and one of her favorite classes was a philosophy of religion class in which the teacher, a physician and minister, taught the students to seek "mindfulness." The class was one and a half hours long, Monday through Friday, and the students often finished their sessions with meditation. On the last day of class, Allie asked the teacher, "How can I take these feelings and what I've learned home?"

The teacher paused, and said, "Why not meditate on that question and you will find an answer." Allie left the class and began a walking meditation just to clear her mind, as well as to experience the peacefulness of the meditation process. She began to think about the last class and some of the commitments made by the students.

In the last class, the students signed a *willingness agreement* to be mindful of the three mindfulness training statements of Thich Nhat Hanh, and most of the students sincerely want to protect the lives of people, plants, and animals. Josh said, "I am going to volunteer at the local animal shelter and wash cars with some of my friends to raise money for a donation to the shelter." Tim added, "That's great to care for animals, but I want to take care of plants. There is this neat gardener who works in our city park for free, and I'm going to ask him if I can help." The teacher nodded and said, "That certainly responds to the first mindfulness training of caring for plants and animals, what about people?" Emily quickly responded, "I could share my time with people in a retirement home; you know, read to them and just be there. That meets the first mindfulness training, and the second one of sharing your time with people and cultivating loving kindness."

It was obvious to the teacher that the students were not only applying the mindfulness training they had discussed in class, but they were validating the experience with one another and with him. They sincerely wanted to continue to practice their mindfulness at home. He paused and asked, "What about the third mindfulness training of mindful speech and the ability to do deep listening?"

After a few minutes, Sam said, "I can use that with my younger brother, and I can quit being on his case all the time." The other students laughed. All of them agreed they could model speaking truthfully, and several added stepping back from gossip, which is damaging to everyone. The teacher listened to their statements, noticed their intense expressions, and said, "Find other people to work with you on your commitments, because so often we have good intentions and fail to follow-through."

The students hugged their teacher and one another, then they went back to the residence hall to pack and head out for home. Allie was flying home and she needed to catch a ride to the airport. Sam asked his mother to drop Allie off at the airport, and they promised to keep in touch via e-mail. On the plane, Allie closed her eyes and began to meditate using the insight meditation and focusing on the question: How can I be a model for loving kindness?

Her first thought was: Use your loving hands. Allie pondered this thought and decided to ask her homeroom teacher if she could present an idea for a committee project to the student council. The teacher agreed and said the student council would be meeting the following week.

Allie sat down at her computer and entered the three mindfulness training statements to print out for the members of the student council. Then she added her idea for a Loving Hands Committee, a group of students who would identify projects to address the three mindfulness training activities.

When Allie approached the student council meeting room, she felt her heart beating, and she was as nervous as she had ever been, even in cheerleading tryouts or in auditioning for school plays. She took a deep breath and took her seat. The advisor of the student council said, "Before we start our meeting today, one of our students, Allie, wants to share an idea for a new committee activity." Allie stood and began handing out the three mindfulness training statements. She noticed that several of the students looked disinterested, and they weren't reading her handout. She took three deep breaths and began, "I want to propose that the student council create a new committee activity called *Loving Hands*. We could identify projects and involve any students who are willing to work with us." There were a few minutes of silence that felt like hours to Allie, and then the advisor said, "I think that is a great idea, and I'm going to suggest that those of you who want to participate contact Allie. The meeting lasted another fifteen minutes, with discussion of the student council's contribution to the opening ceremony of school, and then the students were dismissed.

As Allie left the room, Mia caught up with her and said, "I like your idea, let's talk about it at lunch, OK?" Then she dashed off. Allie met two other student council members in the cafeteria who asked to help with Loving Hands. One student said, "I can draw loving hands, and we could post them in the homeroom for students to list project ideas."

In the next few weeks, a total of twelve students, four from the student council and eight from the student body, met with Allie whenever they had free time. They identified their first activity: to tutor and to read to children at a shelter for abused women and children. The students made a schedule that provided at least two students Monday–Friday to visit the shelter for an hour after school. The feedback they received from the director of the shelter was very positive. She said, "The children look forward to your visits, and they are doing much better at school." Then she added, "But most important, I see a lot more smiles, not only from children, but from their parents.

Allie continued working with the Loving Hands project throughout her final two years of high school, and the committee planned and implemented numerous activities, including working with a retirement center, the city municipal hospital, a Head Start Program, and the Juvenile Justice Center. After graduation from high school, Allie introduced Loving Hands to her university. Today, she and her husband live in Africa, and they both continue to use Loving Hands concepts in Allie's work as a sociologist and in her husband's work as a hospital administrator.

Importance of Selflessness Experiences

Goldstein (2007) said that through a growing realization of selflessness, you can develop a deepening sense of connection. Allie is representative of many gifted students who want to make a difference. She and the other students involved in Loving Hands could move from the small world of ego-identification in Level I of the Dabrowski Theory of Emotional Development to greater experiences of selflessness, which represent Level IV–V behavior.

PEACE EDUCATION

Numerous colleges and universities provide a peace education focus that incorporates negotiation and conflict resolution. This focus on peace is particularly relevant to gifted students who want to make a difference in today's troubled world.

Universities Offering Peace-Related Programs

Peace-related programs are available at universities in Central and South America, Europe, and North America, including Canada and the United States. At the graduate level, fifteen universities in the United States offer MA programs with a focus on international peace and conflict resolution, conflict analysis and management, and mediating theory and democratic systems. Nova Southeastern University in Ft. Lauderdale, Florida, offers a Ph.D. in dispute resolution, and George Mason University offers a Ph.D. in conflict analysis and resolution.

At the undergraduate level, fifteen colleges and universities provide programs focusing on peace studies and conflict resolution. Catholic University in Washington, DC, focuses on peace and world order studies, and Earlham College in Richmond, Indiana, provides peace and global studies.

Seeds of Peace: Warriors of Hope

John Wallach (2000), an author and journalist, founded Seeds of Peace, a group of forty-six Israeli, Palestinian, and Egyptian teenagers who met in Maine and discussed the conflict raging in their homelands. Wallach believed in reconciliation, and that the future was in young people who could learn to be free to face the future, if they let go of the past. The group ate together and roomed together in dormitories. The objective was to build a basis of understanding and reconciliation among the young people. Since 1993, more than 3,000 young people from twenty-five nations have participated in Seeds of Peace with a deep commitment to conflict resolution. In addition to the original camp in Maine, the organization opened a Seeds of Peace Center in Jerusalem. The Jerusalem center launched an Advanced Coexistence program in which 200 young people from Israel and Palestine meet in different parts on both sides of Jerusalem and throughout the West Bank and Israel. These students have produced award-wining documentary films, and they started programs for younger Arab and Jewish children to build understanding and a belief in peace. Each year the Seeds of Peace students are invited to the White House to share their activities. The students are committed to making a change in their families, communities, and schools, and they say the change will begin with them.

NEGOTIATION AND CONFLICT RESOLUTION

Negotiation and conflict resolution are key components in undergraduate and graduate level peace-related programs. However, a great deal can be accomplished at the elementary, middle, and high school level to resolve student conflicts, prior to higher education. Conflicts include quarrels, disagreements, disputes, and struggles, and they are a natural part of day-to-day life. David Johnson (2003), in *Reaching Out: Interpersonal Effectiveness and Self-Actualization*, said that because there are so many conflicts in life, learning the skills of managing and resolving conflicts is one of the best investments education can make. Gifted students take to negotiation and conflict resolution quite naturally with their advanced communication skills, empathy, and compassion for others.

The main objective in a conflict with another person is to achieve your goal, and also to maintain a good relationship with the other person. It helps to think of the goal and the relationship on a continuum: Is this goal of great importance or can it be sacrificed? Will you work or live with the person you have the conflict with for a short time, or is it a long-term relationship? Thinking about this aspect of the conflict at the beginning can help you decide how important your goal is and how important the relationship is to you and to the other person (Johnson, 2003).

Benefits of Negotiation and Conflict Resolution

Working through conflicts with negotiation can help to clarify your values, what you stand for, and what your overall attitude is toward problems. In the negotiation process, the focus is on clarifying the problem and identifying issues that need to be considered. A number of positive outcomes are provided by conflicts:

1. Motivation

2. Perspective taking

3. Cognitive reasoning

4. Mastery and retention of material

5. Creativity

6. High quality of problem solving

7. Cohesion

When you are involved in a conflict, there is considerable *motivation* to try and solve the problem. You put aside other activities and focus on identifying the various aspects of the problem that are essential to addressing the issues. Conflicts energize the people involved in the conflict to take action. One important aspect in conflict resolution is *perspective taking*, in which you look at the problem from the point of view of the other person and try to build an awareness and an understanding of their values and ideas. This process moves the negotiation into the *cognitive reasoning* stage, in which there is an attempt to understand the goals of the other person and to examine just how committed you are to the resolution of the conflict. At this time, you can examine your own patterns of behavior and those of the other person for any dysfunctional patterns of behavior. For example, are there certain parts of the problem that you are ignoring, magnifying, or minifying? In preparation for the negotiation, you will need to do your "homework" and to have the facts well in hand to use in the negotiation process; consequently, there is a need for *mastery and retention* of the facts. *Creativity* is called for in this stage, when you think of strategies to propose for a solution of benefit to both of you. This calls for a *high quality of problem solving,* and searching for many ideas to suggest for solution-finding. Last, one major advantage of a conflict is the *cohesion* it builds in the people involved in the conflict, for as the two of you work together to come up with ideas for consideration that will result in a solution that is agreeable to both of you, a feeling of unity and cohesion will develop.

A Model for Decision Making

A useful model for decision making includes making sure that you know what your *rationale* is in the conflict. What is it that both of you believe to be the facts? Why do you see a conflict? Then during the negotiation, both sides will need to look for a pattern of behavior. What are the underlying causes of the conflict? And how do both people interact in the negotiation? Last, what are the consequences of any proposed solutions? From this decision-making process, action can be taken.

A model for action decision making for conflict resolution developed in a conflict negotiation workshop for the Creative Education Foundation (Sisk, 1989) is illustrated in Figure 9.1.

NEGOTIATION CONFLICT RESOLUTION STRATEGIES

Five negotiation conflict resolution strategies with easy to remember names were suggested by Johnson (2003) and provide a "fun" aspect to the negotiation process. The first strategy is the *turtle,* who withdraws from the conflict, avoiding the other person and the issue just like a turtle that pulls its head into the shell. The second strategy is the *shark,* who forces a point of view, regardless of the consequences of the resolution. The third is the *teddy bear* strategy, in which there is a smoothing and allowing the other person to have his or her way. The fourth is the *fox,* who compromises and gives up part of the goal or relationship to solve the problem. The fifth strategy is the *owl*, who problem solves and negotiates so that both parties can achieve their goals and the relationship can survive.

When the goal is not so important to you in the conflict, you may want to withdraw or *smooth* it over, but when the goal is highly important, you may want to use *force*. However, it is important to evaluate what you may lose by using this strategy. The strategy of *compromise* and *problem solving* can move the conflict toward not only resolving the conflict, but maintaining the relationship between the two people.

Figure 9.1   A Model for Action Decision Making for Conflict Resolution

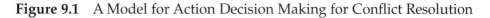

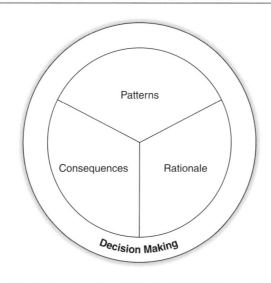

Five Types of Problems That Commonly Create Negative Dynamics in Negotiation

1. Strong emotions
2. Misperceptions or stereotypes
3. Legitimizing problems
4. Lack of trust
5. Poor communication

When two people are involved in a conflict, emotions need to be expressed so that both sides understand how the problem is affecting them. Yet, it is essential that the emotions of the two people in conflict be controlled, for when one individual is angry or resentful, it is very difficult for any compromise to be identified or negotiated. Misperceptions or stereotypes are deadly in negotiation and conflict resolution. For example, what if one person has the perception that people from certain socioeconomic backgrounds or cultures can't be trusted. Whatever the stereotype or misperception that exists, it will become the "lens" through which the two people view one another. Legitimatizing the problems is essential, for if either person in the negotiation thinks that the problem is trivial, or not an important concern, then he or she will approach the problem with a limiting mind-set. Trust is essential in negotiation and conflict resolution. It is important that the people in the conflict trust one another, and most important that they trust the mediator. Communication is very important and each person in the conflict needs to clearly communicate ideas and to have sufficient time to state his or her position without being interrupted.

Mediation Framework

The six steps in a mediation framework include the following:

1. Opening statement
2. Uninterrupted time
3. The exchange
4. Building the agreement
5. Writing the agreement
6. Closing statement

In the mediation framework, these six steps can be used to frame the negotiation process. The first is the *opening statement* made by the mediator in which he or she stresses that the two people involved in the conflict will deal with the conflict in a problem-solving process, and the importance of working together to cooperate in reaching an agreement that will be beneficial to both people. Second, the mediator emphasizes that each person will have *uninterrupted time* to state his or her case, what it is that both people want, and the reason behind the goal or request. Third, during the *exchange* phase, the mediator will try to clarify the differences between the two people in conflict and identify ways that might lead to a compromise. The mediator will focus on what the differences are and where the goals and desires are similar, as well as on actions of either person that could be considered acceptable or unacceptable. Fourth, as they move toward *building an agreement*, the mediator will identify several possible solutions that have emerged during the interchange that may be reasonable in satisfying both people. Once there is an agreement on a solution, the fifth step is to *write the agreement*. The sixth is when the mediator makes a *closing statement* that points out the joint benefit of the proposed solution and includes praise and recognition of the work of the two people in finding a viable solution.

Role of the Mediator

The mediator is responsible for preventing interruptions or verbal attacks, as well as for encouraging the people to focus on the problem and not on each other. Another essential role of the mediator is to translate value-laden or judgmental language into less emotionally charged terms. It is also important that the mediator affirm clear descriptions or statements, and demonstrate the ability to accept the expression of feelings.

In every relationship that you have, you decide on how you want to manage the conflicts that arise. When you are faced with a conflict, you have two concerns, how to achieve your goal and how to maintain the relationship with the other person. Gifted students can profit from serving as a mediator in conflicts at school and at home. In these situations, they can learn to clarify misconceptions and stereotypes, to help summarize the solution that has been agreed upon, and to develop patience as they assist the two people in conflict to reach a decision through problem-solving negotiation that both people are going to be satisfied with and willing to put into action.

Learning to Negotiate

Sisk and Shallcross (1986) in *Leadership: Making Things Happen* said the first thing to decide on in negotiation is if the problem can be negotiated. Are the two people involved in the problem of equal power? Is there something or some idea that can be bargained with in the negotiation? They suggest an activity that gifted students can use to learn how to negotiate, called "What Do You Want?"

What Do You Want?

In successfully completing your negotiation, what would you want to accomplish? Specify dollars, quantities, delivery dates, payment terms, and all other aspects of your ideal objectives. What would your negotiation look like if you got everything you wanted?

_____

_____

_____

Now that you have completed your objectives, anticipate your opponent's point of view. Try to move away from your own goals and try to think of the other person. What do you think they would want?

_____

_____

_____

Now that you have done some preliminary thinking about your negotiation, what will you talk about? What are the issues? What are you willing to concede or suggest? Make an agenda. What do you want to talk about first, second, and third?

_____

_____

_____

Agenda

1. _____

2. _____

3. _____

(Sisk & Shallcross, 1986, pp. 115–116)

An Example of Negotiation

Negotiation isn't always between people; it can be between groups, such as a conflict between a group of third grade students and a group of fifth grade students. The third grade students have the same recess period as the fifth grade students, and each day the older students manage to take the kick ball from the younger group of students. The third grade students said to their teacher, "It's not right. They take the ball away from us each day, and that's not fair." The teacher agreed and said, "Why don't we try some negotiation skills with them?" Several students looked perplexed, and Jon asked the teacher, "What does negotiation mean?" The teacher chuckled and said, "It's a skill that you can learn to help you get what you want, and still be friends with the fifth grade boys and girls."

At this point, the teacher wrote on the overhead projector, *What Do You Want?* And she asked the students to tell her what their objectives would be. They said, "We want to have fun at recess." "We want to play dodge ball during recess." "We want to play kick ball in teams."

Then she wrote on the overhead: What do you think the fifth grade students want? The children said, "They want to play kick ball just like us? They want to play dodge ball too." "They want to have fun at recess."

The teacher pointed to the list for the fifth grade students, and then to their list, and asked the students, "Aren't the two lists alike?" They reluctantly agreed. Then the teacher said, "Let's think of some solutions to our problem that would be acceptable for both our class and theirs." Why don't you get into groups of five and come up with some ideas. After about ten minutes, the teacher asked the students to share their ideas.

Tim said, "We could ask the principal to buy another ball." Jon added, "We could use the ball on Monday and Tuesday, and they could use it in on Thursday and Friday." "What about Wednesday?" the teacher asked. The students laughed and said, "We could challenge the fifth graders to a dodge ball or a kick ball game, and we could beat them!"

The teacher said, "You know that isn't such a bad idea. What do you think?" The students agreed that it was a possibility, but they liked the idea of the principal buying another ball as well. The teacher said, "I will speak to the principal and see what he says. And I will ask the fifth grade teacher to see if her students would be willing to share the ball, and have a day in which the two grades could play a game together." She paused and said, "I would like one of you to go with me and present our ideas to the class." Several students said, "Let Jon go with you; his sister is in the class and that might help." Jon agreed, and he and the teacher presented the ideas to the fifth grade class. The fifth grade class agreed with the ideas, and one student said, "Part of the fun of taking the ball away from you is having you chase us for it." Another student said, "On Wednesday, we will beat you at dodge ball or kick ball." The two teachers looked at one another, and later both agreed that the students had learned a great deal about negotiation and the give-and-take in conflict resolution.

Negotiable Issues Versus Nonnegotiable Issues

Johnson (2003) suggested an exercise for students to use in learning how to negotiate in which they list issues that are negotiable and issues that are nonnegotiable, such as eating a pizza or shoplifting. Then he suggested the students role-play someone asking them to do something that is nonnegotiable. Students usually list nonnegotiable issues such as cheating on a test, stealing someone's lunch, writing graffiti on the school walls, bringing guns to school, hurting little kids, and lying. Johnson said that activities like these not only help the students to clarify their values, but they provide the teachers information about their students that can be used in guiding them in making constructive decisions.

Engaging Gifted Students as Mediators in School Conflicts

Silverman (1993), in a chapter titled "Techniques for Preventive Counseling" in the book *Counseling the Gifted and Talented,* points out that the experiences gifted students have had in creative problem solving can help them be successful in conflict resolution. Gifted students can list as many alternatives as possible to help deal with the problem, and Silverman stressed that gifted students need to learn how to ask for what they want and to work toward a win-win situation. The following example of gifted students functioning as negotiators demonstrates their ability to use their communication skills, creativity, and willingness to serve.

CASE STUDY

The counselor at a middle school was plagued with small conflicts between students on a daily basis that were taking a great deal of her time, time that she wanted to spend on more serious problems. She decided to approach the Supervisor of Gifted Education with the idea of teaching several of the high school gifted students to be mediators for conflict resolution in the middle school. The high school was located across the street from the middle school, which would provide easy access to the middle school. The counselor and supervisor asked the seniors if they would be willing to work as mediators in a negotiation process with the middle school students, that they would receive training and it would require volunteer time of forty-five minutes a week, which would count toward service points needed for graduation. Ten of the seniors said they would be willing to function as mediators. The Johnson (2003) book, *Reaching Out: Interpersonal Effectiveness and Self-Actualization*, was used as a resource, and the students spent several homeroom periods role-playing several of the suggested activities in the chapter on resolving interpersonal conflicts. In addition, the students role-played several current conflicts happening in their high school between different student groups. The student-mediators used the format introduced in this chapter to work with the middle school students. They started with an opening statement such as:

> I am here today to work with the two of you, Yolanda and Tara, on the conflict that you have over the damage to Yolanda's cell phone. Each of you will have five minutes of uninterrupted time to share your side of the conflict, and then we will have an exchange in which you can ask each other questions. Then we will try and build an agreement with solutions that both of you can agree on and accept. Then we will write an agreement that both of you can sign. Last, I will make some closing statements.

The mediator, Amy, and the students followed the format, and they said the conflict involved Yolanda being pushed into a swimming pool by Tara, and Yolanda's cell phone, which was in her pocket, was ruined. Tara said she was just having fun and didn't know the cell phone was in Yolanda's pocket. As the students described the incident, much of their anger was diffused and the two girls began to come up with solutions. They listed:

1. Tara could buy Yolanda a new phone.

2. Tara could give Yolanda her cell phone.

3. Yolanda could use Tara's phone at school.

4. Tara could babysit and give money to Yolanda to buy a phone.

5. Tara could apologize for ruining the cell phone.

6. Tara and Yolanda could have a rummage sale of stuff they didn't want, like old CDs, books, and toys, and use the money to buy a cell phone.

7. Yolanda could use her mom's old cell phone.

8. Yolanda and Tara could look for "bargains" in the newspaper for cell phones.

As the girls listed the ideas, their voices became softer, and the student-mediator recorded this in her notes. She asked the girls if they were ready to examine the eight ideas that had been generated, and to see if there were any solutions listed that both could accept. The two girls liked the idea of checking for bargains in the newspaper, #8, and Tara said she could do #5 now. "I am so sorry," she said. "I didn't mean to ruin your phone." And she added, "I like the idea of a rummage sale, what do you think?" Yolanda agreed that #6 was a good idea, so the student-mediator asked them to write an agreement.

They wrote: "We will have a rummage sale and use the money we earn to buy a cell phone, after checking for bargains in the paper."

The student-mediator made the following closing statement:

I was impressed with your ability to think of solutions to your problem, and you worked well together without being angry. I also thought Tara apologizing in front of me was great; that took a lot of courage. I think your idea of a rummage sale with both of you working together is sort of a symbol of a good negotiation. Also, let me know when your rummage sale is going to be held, and I will bring some of my friends to support you.

Amy, the student-mediator, shared the problem and the agreement with the counselor and the Supervisor of Gifted Education and she said, "Working with the two middle school students on their conflict was a great experience for me; I want to be a lawyer and it helped me think about the aspects of a conflict in a whole different light. I will be more than willing to continue being a student-mediator."

Benefits of Negotiation and Conflict Resolution for Gifted Students

Conflicts end when an agreement is reached in which both people are comfortable and satisfied with the solution. Negotiation can be used in conflicts at home and in school, and the most important part of negotiation is that the two people in conflict problem solve together so that both are satisfied with the agreement. It is essential that gifted students learn how to articulate what it is that they want and to identify their feelings around the conflict, and, most important, to recognize their reasons for wanting what they want and why they feel the way they do. Gifted students can be very strong in their opinions and they are often classified by both parents and teachers as stubborn. Learning how to negotiate is a skill that can be a lifetime skill for living peacefully with others, and learning to take the perspective of others can eliminate many misunderstandings before they become conflicts, which can help to make life much more tranquil.

SUMMARY

In this chapter, we explored the concept that peace begins with the individual and examined ways that a sense of peace and tranquility can be introduced to gifted students. Practical applications of Thich Nhat Hanh were explored including meditation. The Sanskrit word *maitri* and the Pali word *metta* that mean loving kindness were discussed, along with the ideas of Joseph Goldstein for practicing loving kindness for oneself and for all. An example of a second grade teacher using loving kindness practices was provided, and Goldstein said practicing loving kindness changes the way you relate to the world.

Hanh stressed the importance of focusing on your breathing, and his suggestion for a "Today's Day" was examined in which the earth could be honored. An example of a first grade teacher using the idea of a Today's Day with her class was introduced. Mindfulness was defined as the seed of enlightenment including awareness, understanding, care, compassion, liberation, transformation and healing by Thich Nhat Hanh. One of his activities, Flower Watering, used in the Plum Village was illustrated that provides an opportunity for building community and focusing on positive affirmation.

Three of the Mindfulness Training activities were discussed as a set of guidelines that can be used with gifted students in a Peace Education focus in Social Studies, in an enrichment program, or in a service learning project. The instinct for compassion was introduced with examples provided by Goleman (2006) of Princeton Seminary students taking part in an experiment of compassion and altruism that indicated students who are self-absorbed are less likely to assist an injured individual. This was in contrast to rhesus monkeys that demonstrated an automatic impulse to try to help a monkey who was shocked when they pulled a lever for food.

Meditation was defined as an internal process of discovering and becoming familiar with your mind, including insight meditation and walking meditation. The work of Rozman in meditation with children was discussed, and an example of a Spaceship Meditation was provided. A case study was provided of a gifted student who developed a Loving Kindness project while in high school, continued it in college, and still uses it in her work in Africa, along with her husband. Allie is a wonderful example of the selflessness that Goldstein described as a way to build a growing sense of connection with others.

Ways of developing a sense of peace and tranquility were examined including peace education programs provided at the university and college level. These programs emphasize negotiation and conflict resolution as part of their curriculum. The benefits of conflict resolution were discussed, and a model for decision making was provided, along with the negotiation and conflict resolution strategies of Johnson (2003), including the turtle, the shark, the teddy bear, the fox, and the owl. Types of problems that create negative dynamics in negotiation were highlighted and a mediation framework was outlined. The role of the mediator was discussed and activities to assist gifted students in learning to negotiate were provided. An example of negotiation between a third and fifth grade group of students was examined, and another example of high school gifted students functioning as student-mediators in conflict resolution with middle school students in a school setting was provided. A conflict ends when both parties are satisfied with the agreement, and the importance of gifted students learning how to negotiate as a skill that can be a lifetime skill to enable them to live peacefully with others was stressed.

Teacher Voice

I truly believe, as the chapter says, peace begins with the individual. Sometimes in my class, the gifted students are so full of energy that it is difficult for them to focus, so I take them outside (even my high school kids) and get them involved in observing and thinking about nature, whether it is gathering materials to build a simulated bird's nest with tweezers like a bird, or just filling in I Notice/I Wonder sheets to strengthen their observation skills. These activities build their "mindfulness" for protecting the environment that was introduced in Thich Nhat Hanh's mindfulness training. I liked the negotiation and conflict activities, and I am going to suggest them to our counselor. I know our kids could benefit from helping others solve conflicts, and I plan to share what the college students (Eli and Freddie) were doing, so my students can be inspired to identify projects they could carry out to become instruments of peace. I would like to see peace education focus in all of our gifted classes. I say, "If you take the time to truly see the heart of each of your gifted students, and you don't see peace and tranquility, then you need to focus on the environment of your classroom, and use soothing music, and provide some quiet reflective time." My last reflection is on the importance of helping gifted kids set realistic goals, and then guide them through the steps of Aaron to ensure success for them in reaching their goals.

Terri Clark
Ninth/tenth grade teacher

Read On

Gilman, B. (2003). *Empowering gifted minds: Advocacy that works.* Denver, CO: DeLeon.

Matthews, D., & Foster, J. (2007). *Being smart about gifted children.* Scottsdale, AZ: Great Potential Press.

Ruf, D. (2005). *Losing our minds: Gifted children left behind.* Scottsdale, AZ: Great Potential Press.

Silverman, L. (2002). Asynchronous development. In M. Neihart, S. Reis, M. Robinson, & S. Moon (Eds.), *The social and emotional development of gifted children: What do we know?* (pp. 31–37). Waco, TX: Prufrock Press.

Smutny, J. (2001). *Stand up for your gifted child: How to make the most of kids' strengths at school and at home.* Minneapolis, MN: Free Spirit.

Log On

The Mindfulness Bell (http://www.iamhome.org/). A worldwide directory of the practice of mindfulness.

Open Space Communications (http://www.openspacecom.com/). This Web site can provide back issues of *Understanding Our Gifted,* covering social and emotional issues of gifted students.

Successconsciousness.com (http://www.successconsciousness.com/books/peace-of-mind-in-daily-life.htm). This Web site provides a chapter from the book, *Peace of Mind in Daily Life* by Remez Sasson.

Reflect On

- Think about conflicts that you have had over the past few years. List two or three of the conflicts with family, friends, or coworkers and the feelings you experienced, as well as the strategies you used in resolving each conflict. Do you see a pattern?
- When you still yourself and meditate, what are some of the problems you have in clearing your mind? Does walking meditation work for you?
- When you negotiate, are you more apt to use the strategy of a turtle or a shark? Do you use the fox and the owl? What about the teddy bear? Do you use different strategies with your family than you use with your friends? Why?
- A school usually benefits if the students, faculty, and staff can reconcile their differences. Think of a recent conflict and your role in resolving the conflict. How important is it to you to contribute to the welfare of your school community?

REFERENCES

Dabrowski, K., & Piechowski, W. (1997). *Theories of levels of emotional development.* Oceanside, NY: Dabor Science.

Darwin, C. (1998). *The descent of man.* Princeton, NJ: Princeton University Press.

Farrer-Halls, G. (2000). *The illustrated encyclopedia of Buddhist wisdom.* Wheaton, IL. Theosophical Publishing.

Germer, C. (2007). Getting along: Loving the other without losing your self. *Tricycle,* Spring, 25–27.

Gilman, B. (2003). *Empowering gifted minds: Advocacy that works.* Denver, CO: DeLeon.

Goldstein, J. (2007). *A heart full of peace.* Boston: Wisdom Publications.

Goleman, D. (2006). *Social intelligence.* New York: Random House.

Hanh, T. (1992). *Touching peace: Practicing the art of mindful living.* Berkeley, CA: Parallax Press.

Hanh, T. (2005). *Being peace.* Berkeley, CA: Parallax Press.

Johnson, D. (2003). *Reaching out: Interpersonal effectiveness and self-actualization.* Boston: Allyn & Bacon.

Matthews, D., & Foster, J. (2007). *Being smart about gifted children.* Scottsdale, AZ: Great Potential Press.

Miller, N. (2006, November 1). *Developmental dynamisms.* Paper presented at the National Association for Gifted, Charlotte, NC.

Rozman, D. (1988). *Meditating with children: The art of concentration and centering.* Boulder Creek, CO: University of the Trees Press.

Ruf, D. (2005). *Losing our minds: Gifted children left behind.* Scottsdale, AZ: Great Potential Press.

Silverman, L. (1993). Techniques for preventive counseling. In L. Silverman (Ed.), *Counseling the gifted and talented* (pp. 81–109). Denver, CO: Love.

Silverman, L. (1998). Through the lens of gifted. *Roeper Review, 20,* 209–210.

Silverman, L. (2002). Asynchronous development. In M. Neihart, S. Reis, M. Robinson, & S. Moon (Eds.), *The social and emotional development of gifted children: What do we know?* (pp. 31–37). Waco, TX: Prufrock Press.

Sisk, D. (1989, June). *Decision-making for conflict resolution.* Paper presented at the Creative Problem Solving Institute, Buffalo, NY.

Sisk, D., & Shallcross, D. (1986) *Leadership: Making things happen.* Buffalo, NY: Bearly.

Smutny, J. (2001). *Stand up for your gifted child: How to make the most of kids' strengths at school and at home.* Minneapolis, MN: Free Spirit.

Wallach, J. (2000). *The enemy has a face: The seeds of peace experience.* Washington, DC: U.S. Institute of Peace Press.

10

Achieving Balance in Your Life and Finding Your Purpose

A synchrony means being "out of sync" or out of balance, both internally in the rates of cognitive, emotional, and physical development and externally in relation to age mates and age norms. Linda Silverman, a psychologist and director of the Gifted Development Center in Denver, Colorado, discussed the experience of being out of sync in a keynote address of the eleventh World Conference of Gifted and Talented Children in Hong Kong. She stressed that an examination of the normal curve of intelligence indicates the majority of the population (68 percent) are within one standard deviation of 100 IQ, and that each standard deviation in either direction places the student at-risk for peer rejection and lack of fit with the rate of learning in the regular classroom and in social relations (Silverman, 1998).

Stephanie Tolan, author and parent of a highly gifted child, in a discussion on asynchrony, said asynchrony is even more complex when the psychological factors are considered. She said the gifted child is an amalgam of developmental stages and that he or she may appear to be different ages in different situations (Tolan, 1989).

AMALGAM OF DEVELOPMENTAL STAGES

An example of this amalgam of developmental stages is 5-year-old Simon, who leaned forward eagerly responding to all of the questions being asked during a Stanford Binet Intelligence examination, in which he achieved an IQ of 155. During the testing, Simon was self-confident, quick to respond, and articulate. Yet, when his mother was asked to come in for a consultation with the psychologist, Simon climbed into her lap, plucked at her jacket, and whined, "I'm ready to go home." In the testing situation, Simon responded according to his mental age of eight years and two months, but when he was tired and eager to go home, he responded according to his chronological age of five years and six months.

In this chapter, we explore the importance of understanding the impact of asynchrony on gifted students and examine brain research that indicates the amygdala can hijack the neocortex or thinking brain, providing the emotions power to disrupt thinking. The challenge is how to balance intellectual and emotional intensity. We examine the concept of being in balance and what being in balance looks like, in comparison to being out of balance. Rushing is discussed as a unique phenomenon of overscheduled gifted kids who need to learn to say "no." The power of purpose is introduced as a strategy to engage gifted students in identifying and in pursuing satisfying work and life styles, as well as dealing with their asynchrony. The use of self-talk to explore aspects of self, and the importance of goal setting in discovering one's purpose and finding meaning in life, are explored. A section on young gifted people making a difference, eminent Nobel Laureate adults, and foundations making a difference offers examples of people with a purpose. The last topic in this chapter focuses on embracing life with a passion and developing a mind-set of positive energy to help others.

IMPORTANCE OF UNDERSTANDING ASYNCHRONY

It is vitally important that parents and teachers understand the impact of asynchrony in gifted students, and help them understand that these differences are normal for them. This task becomes even more complex for parents and teachers when the intensities or overexcitabilities are considered. When intellectual and emotional intensity are paired, this results in gifted children and gifted adults intensely experiencing their daily life.

WHAT DOES BRAIN RESEARCH SAY ABOUT INTELLECTUAL AND EMOTIONAL INTENSITY?

The research of Joseph Le Doux, a neuroscientist at the Center for Neural Science of New York University, represents groundbreaking work in building an understanding of emotional intensity. In *Synaptic Self: How Our Brains Become Who We Are,* Le Doux (2002) explains how the amygdala can take control over what we do even as the prefrontal cortex or "thinking brain" is processing the information to come to a decision (Figure 10.1). Le Doux is a pioneer in working on the key role of the amygdala. He was the first to work out neural pathways for feelings that bypass the neocortex and how those feelings take the direct route through the amygdala. In his research with rats, Le Doux discovered a small bundle of neurons that led directly from the thalamus to the amygdala, in addition to those going through the larger path of neurons to the neocortex.

Daniel Goleman (1996) in *Emotional Intelligence* described how the amygdala can have us springing to action while the slightly slower—but more fully informed—neocortex is unfolding a more well-thought-out plan for action. This emotional hijacking mechanism of the amygdala provides the emotions power to disrupt thinking; consequently, the challenge for us is how to harmonize or balance our intellectual intensity and emotional intensity.

New and exciting research is being conducted at the Laboratory for Affective Neuroscience by Richard Davidson at the University of Wisconsin in Madison. Davidson (2004) has found in his studies of "brain maps" of neural terrain that meditation can produce a significant increase in activity in the part of the brain responsible for positive emotions and traits like optimism and resilience. This would suggest that you could assist your fretful mind in responding in a more positive manner.

Gifted kids often report being "frazzled" or coming "unglued" with their emotions, which keeps them from fully functioning intellectually. When this occurs, refocusing can help them to regain their equilibrium and manage their emotions. Simply and slowly counting to ten, doing the

Figure 10.1 Brain—Prefrontal Cortex and Amygdala

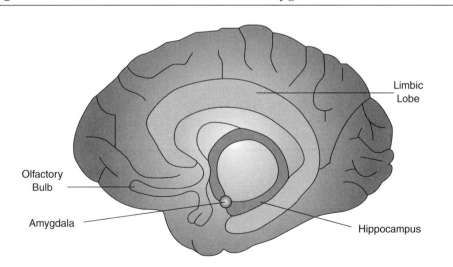

Source: Barry Nix, Central Magnet Medical School, Beaumont, Texas.

deep breathing and meditating suggested by Thich Nhat Hanh, or making a conscious choice to stop "feeling" and becoming aware of the choice can also help them to refocus. They can use visualization and see a soothing scene in their mind's eye to help calm the emotional intensity.

On the other hand, gifted kids can use their senses to become totally "absorbed" by listening to music, enjoying or creating art, and taking a walk to experience nature. The process of refocusing or shifting their focus allows gifted kids to call in their emotions to enrich intellectual activities or to calm their emotions so they can more fully function intellectually. To accomplish refocusing, there is an inference that individuals have the quality of resilience. Schlessinger (2006) said resilience implies that you are motivated not only to make things better, but you are willing to form trusting relationships that are nurturing. Talking to parents, friends, teachers, and counselors can help gifted kids to develop a more coherent view of themselves.

Gifted students have a number of characteristics to help support them, including critical thinking, creativity, inventiveness, and willingness to explore who they are to achieve balance in their life, and to use the energy of their overexcitabilities to seek self-knowledge and self-actualization.

When gifted kids are out of balance, they may experience the following:

- Ongoing fatigue
- Emotional numbness
- Irritability
- Mood swings
- Psychosomatic symptoms
- Acid reflux

For gifted students, or anyone who is out of balance, it is helpful to indulge or treat oneself. This can include activities that intuitively raise positive energy, such as singing, enjoying a rainbow or a sunset, or dancing. It is clear when these activities are working, because you will feel "right" deep down in your core of being. When gifted kids are balanced, they will experience the following:

- Excitement
- Physical stamina
- Patience
- Emotional balance
- Passion

In seeking balance, gifted kids need to be counseled on how to say "no" and to make room for quality personal time. Balance in life means the presence of self-control and discipline, as well as the ability not to let outside events influence their emotions, actions, and reactions. It is also important for them to remember that not everything needs to be done today and to enjoy doing what they "relish."

RUSHING

Gifted students are often overscheduled with multiple overlapping activities. The character Hermione Granger in the Harry Potter books is a splendid example of overscheduling, and the intellectual and emotional intensity of gifted kids. She can distort time and be in two places at the same time, enabling her to attend two simultaneous classes. The problem with such "rushing" is that your energy gets scattered, and your ability to listen is impaired, as well as your memory for details. Rushing is defined in Webster's dictionary as a violent forward motion, to act with haste in a short time at a high speed. Gifted kids can learn to stop and take five minutes from their usual thinking, sit comfortably, take a few deep breaths, and then direct their attention inward. Orloff (2004) in *Positive Energy* suggests two questions that can be helpful in thinking about the impact of rushing: (1) Does my pace feel good? (2) How does my pacing at school feel? At home?

THE POWER OF PURPOSE

Gifted students ponder such deep questions as "Why am I here?" "What do I do with my life?" "What are my gifts?" and "How can I make a difference?" The importance of purpose was captured by George Bernard Shaw:

> This is the true joy in life, being used for a purpose recognized by yourself as a mighty one; being thoroughly worn out before you are thrown on the scrap heap; being a force of nature instead of a feverish little clod of ailments and grievances complaining that the world will not devote itself to making you happy. (Shaw, 1905, p. xxxi)

Leider (1997), founding partner of the Inventure Group, a training firm in Minneapolis, Minnesota, helps individuals and teams discover the power of purpose. He interviewed older adults (over 65) with questions similar to the questions gifted kids ponder, focusing on two questions: "What am I trying to do with my life?" and specifically, "If you could live your life over again, what would you do differently?" He combined their responses and his experience in the fields of adult development and counseling psychology to write *The Power of Purpose: Creating Meaning in Your Life and Work*. From the interviews, the following three themes emerged:

1. Be more reflective.

2. Be more courageous.

3. Be clear earlier about purpose.

Leider concluded from the interviews that all people seem to have a natural desire and capacity to contribute to life, and for gifted kids and adults that desire is magnified. He stressed that the key to acting on purpose is to bring together the needs of the world with your unique gifts in a vocation or a "calling." Teaching is a calling, and most teachers realize they are the second most important people in the lives of their students, next to their parents and caregivers. Working and living on purpose provides a reason for "being" and it provides a sense of direction. Leider suggested an activity on which gifted kids could journal or just sit quietly and reflect:

> Look ahead, how old do you think you'll live to be? Imagine you're that age. As you look back on your life, what would you like to be able to say is your legacy? Have you become the somebody you were destined to be? What might you do with your remaining time so that you can look back over your life with no regrets? (Leider, 1997, p. 11)

People with a sense of purpose learn to move their focus away from themselves and to focus on others, which represents the higher levels of functioning in the multilevels of Dabrowski (Level IV–V). Level IV individuals are well on the way to self-actualization and Level V individuals live a life in service to humanity.

Finding Your Purpose or Calling

If purpose is defined as the conscious choice of *what*, *where*, and *how* to make a contribution to the community, to the nation, and to the world, the first step according to Leider is to discover your gifts and to identify what moves you to use incredible energy in your life. To find your calling, it is essential that you slow down and go within to tap your inner voice or knowing. That inner voice is your intuition or intuitive thinking. *Intuition: An Inner Way of Knowing* (Sisk & Shallcross, 1989) suggested finding quiet moments in nature and pondering: What are my gifts? What provides me a sense of joy and passion? And how can I bring my gifts and my passion into my life and work?

Journaling is another way to find your purpose. Leider said that if finding your purpose or calling is beyond your reach, you could try a "shorthand version" of finding your purpose for the next day. An example of a 10-year-old gifted boy's journal entry for the next day is as follows:

> My purpose for tomorrow is to finish my science fair project on fruit flies. My project is coming along. I like making the tables and drawings, and I think I want to be a scientist—NO, I want to be a scientist.

When a group of graduate students in gifted education were asked to identify their purpose or calling, one teacher wrote: "My purpose is to help gifted students use their talents and embrace the world—to make it a better place with all of their energy and passion."

Gifted Kids Find Their Calling in Cuba

Several years ago, a group of thirty teachers and administrators of gifted programs from throughout the United States visited Cuba during a People to People Program to meet with teachers and to observe program efforts for Cuba's gifted students. The Cuban teachers said they help their students find a "calling" and then they assist them in fulfilling their calling in music, art, dance, literature, science, and math. The teachers described calling as "following with your heart" (Sisk, 1990).

In discovering your purpose, and more important in living your purpose, it is important to eliminate activities or tasks that take you away from your calling. At the highest level of Dabrowski (Level V), the individual is using his or her talents to make the world a better place. Teachers are making the world a better place as they touch the lives of children and assist them in using their positive energy in finding meaning in life.

EXPLORING ASPECTS OF SELF

Self-talk can be very helpful in exploring aspects of self. Words, thoughts, feelings, impressions, insights, flashes of intuition, or physical responses such as tightness in the chest, butterflies in the stomach, a pain in the stomach, or a headache are all part of self-talk (Aaron, 1991). Our body talks to us and that self-talk becomes our reality. It is important to pay attention to self-talk, such as reflecting on when do those butterflies arrive and with whom? Once the time and the people involved are identified, then efforts can be made to change that reality. Aaron suggested one way to build a greater understanding of self-talk is to keep a record of your self-talk. You could make a list of positive self-talk and identify all of those "atta-boy and atta-girl" statements in your day-to-day life, and then make a list of the negative self-talk, such as "You can't do that; you never could do that." If the lists indicate negative self-talk happens mostly when you are thinking about a new goal or task, you may want to build greater efficacy in goal setting. Alter (2006) in *The Defining Moment* said that if you don't have goals, establish some, and know precisely what they are, then examine how close you are to fulfilling them.

BUILDING EFFICACY IN GOAL SETTING

Efficacy is defined as the ability to make things happen, the power to create and to produce the results you want to have happen. Think about a goal in terms of what you want to accomplish. Then visualize the goal as if it were completed and be aware of how you would feel when the goal is completed. Then repeat the goal to yourself. This process is similar to the affirmation process in that you are sending a message to yourself that it is OK to seek this particular goal. Philip Aaron in *The Power to Create* suggested three steps for goal setting: (1) Clear out the blocks in meeting your goal; (2) Make lists of at least two things you feel are unresolved in each of five categories: personal, physical, emotional, social, and intellectual; and (3) Select one or two of the categories and identify issues that would lead to a definitive goal (Aaron, 1991).

CASE STUDY

Marta is a highly gifted teenager living in a rural community with no provisions for a gifted education program in the school system, and there are few students in Marta's school with similar interests or ability in music and mathematics. Marta wants to accelerate her schooling and seek early entrance to college primarily, as she says, "To do something useful for others and to make a difference." She suffers from an acid reflux condition and severe headaches that the family doctor describes as "school-related." Marta agrees that her headaches are school-related because they happen when the mathematics teacher asks her to work on math problems and processes that she already knows, or in the orchestra when she is forced to play simple musical pieces on her French horn when she would rather play much more complex music. Marta's school counselor gave her Aaron's book, *The Power to Create*, to read and asked her to list two unresolved problems or issues in the following five categories. She wrote the following:

Personal

1. I want to be able to convince my parents that going to college early is possible.

2. I need to be more independent so my parents and teachers will see me as capable of going to school early.

Physical

1. I need to watch what I eat and learn how to stay calm to get rid of the acid reflux.

2. I need to set my own alarm clock so Mom won't have to wake me up in the morning; then she will see me as responsible and that I can do that for myself in college.

Emotional

1. I need to work on not being so sensitive. My feelings get hurt when people make fun of my vocabulary, my "big words," and my dreams to make a difference.

2. I would describe myself as shy, and I don't speak up for myself.

Intellectual (School)

1. My grades aren't that good in school, mostly because the assignments are so dumb and I just don't complete them.

2. I am a real perfectionist—when I work on something, I want it to be just right.

After listing her unresolved issues, Marta identified several issues on which she could focus: (1) Becoming more independent, (2) Taking responsibility for her diet, (3) Being more assertive, and (4) Improving her grades to build a better case for early entrance to college.

Marta stated her goal as: I see myself in college, being independent, using good task management, and getting good grades.

Aaron (1991) suggested that goals need to be written in present tense and in positive language, and Marta's goal meets both of these criteria.

Joseph Campbell and Bill Moyers in *The Power of Myth* (1988) stressed the importance of finding your bliss, and said that when you do, you will begin to meet people who are on the same invisible track and who share your goals. Marta met a young man, Justin, who attends her church, and he shared being in dual enrollment in high school and junior college so he would have enough college credits on graduation from high school to enter college as a sophomore. When Marta heard this, she made an appointment with her school counselor, who then made arrangements for her to enroll in an Algebra II class at the junior college. Marta's mother noticed she was awakening herself in the morning and seldom complained of headaches. Justin invited Marta to attend a junior college open house, and then doors began to open for her. She finished her senior year simultaneously with her first year of junior college and achieved her goal. As she enthusiastically said, "Achieving my goal wasn't the most important outcome; the real outcome was discovering my own power—there are people and children with dreams that will die without a helping hand, and I want a cause."

FINDING MEANING IN LIFE

Finding meaning in life is another way to bring balance into your life, and you can find meaning in life when you creatively achieve a task. Aaron (1991) suggested making a list of tasks that you have done or observed other people doing that don't seem to make sense because they lack meaning. Then, make a list of tasks that have meaning for you and do some "self-talk" to identify why each of the tasks were listed as either with meaning or without meaning.

Tasks With Meaning or Without Meaning

Tasks with little or no meaning   No meaning because

_____   _____

Tasks with much meaning   Much meaning because

_____   _____

If your life is full of meaningless tasks, you either need to find value and meaning in them or change yourself or change your tasks (Aaron, 1991).

Marta completed this exercise with her school counselor and listed "Showing the work behind a math problem" as a task with no meaning. Then she listed "Taking care of my baby sister so my mother can finish dinner" as a task with meaning. Marta's reason for showing the work or proofs of math problems as having no meaning was, "It wastes my time." Her reason for her task with much meaning was, "I enjoy being responsible for Caitlin and helping my mom."

The challenge for Marta was to see how showing proofs for her math problems could improve her scores in math, which represented her goal to get better grades to enter college early. As Marta's parents and counselor observed her commitment and eagerness for seeking early entrance to college, as well as her growing responsibility and resolve to make changes in her behavior, they began to compliment her goal-directed behavior. Most people enjoy receiving praise and approval, which encourages them to seek further successes, and Marta was no exception. She became more highly motivated to achieve her goal and demonstrated a willingness to work toward reaching it. Gifted kids like Marta want to make a difference, and by becoming aware of their talents, finding their passion and discovering their purpose, they can find a form of service that moves them.

FINDING VALUE AND MEANING IN LIFE

In 1835, Alexis de Tocqueville (1994) noted in his book *Democracy in America* the eagerness of Americans to bond together in community groups to attack common problems. This observation still holds true today, as individuals seek to find value and meaning in their life by making a difference. We live in an interdependent world and consequently we cannot escape each other's problems. We are all vulnerable to terror, the spread of disease, and the potentially calamitous effects of climate change. The challenge for our gifted young people and for all of us is how to reach across the "divides" of our interdependent world and create shared opportunities and shared responsibilities (Gore, 2006).

Students Making a Difference

Eli Winkelman, a student at Scripps College in southern California, formed her own organization called Challah for Hunger. Each week Challah for Hunger volunteers produce more than 150 loaves of challah, the braided bread that is traditionally broken at the beginning of the Sabbath meal in Jewish homes. Each Friday, the students sell the bread on tables where they also display material on the hunger crisis in Darfur. Since 2004, Eli and the students have donated more than $20,000 from Scripps and other colleges in the Clermont group to Darfur. The efforts of the group have expanded to the University of Texas in Austin and to the University of Massachusetts in Amherst. Challah for Hunger represents a Jewish effort for poor Muslims, and Eli's business card has a quote from Rabbi Tarfon: "You are not obligated to complete the task, but you are not free to withdraw from it."

Another student effort in making a difference is the work of Freddi Zeiler, a University of California at Berkeley student. She wrote *A Kid's Guide to Giving* with the support of By Kids for Kids, an organization working to develop the innovative spirit in all kids. Her book lists why you should give, how to choose a cause, and how to contribute money, time, and things. In addition, there is a summary analysis of the needs of people, animals, and the environment.

Eli Winkelman and Freddi Zeiler are examples of individuals who are making a difference, and they can serve as role models and sources of information to gifted students who want to make a difference.

Adults Who Are Making a Difference

President Jimmy Carter won the Nobel Peace Prize in 2002, primarily for his work after leaving the White House. He was lauded for fighting to eradicate guinea worm and river blindness in Africa, helping poor nations to become self-sufficient in food production, promoting human rights, building homes with Habitat for Humanity, and monitoring elections in troubled democracies to make sure that all eligible citizens can vote and that their votes are counted.

In 2004, the Nobel Peace Prize was awarded to another citizen activist, Wangari Maathai of Kenya. She was the first East African woman to earn a doctoral degree, and she is an environmentalist. The prize was awarded for her tree-planting effort to provide soil and water conservation, sustainable development, the empowerment of women, and for promoting good governance and peace. The work of Maathai has evolved into the Green Belt Movement, and her goal is to plant one billion trees over the next decade (Maathai, 2006).

The Nobel Peace Prize was awarded to Muhammad Yunus of Bangladesh in 2006. He founded the Grameen Bank, which makes loans to poor people, and 97 percent of the loans are to women. In a nation with a per capita annual income of less than $500, the Grameen Bank has made nearly seven million loans since 1983. These loans were made without requiring collateral or even a signed agreement. Yunus reports a loan recovery of 98.3 percent and that by 2007 more than 58 percent of the Grameen borrowers had lifted themselves above the poverty line (Yunus, 1999; Dowla & Barua, 2006).

Foundations Making a Difference

The Bill and Melinda Gates Foundation has spent more than a billion dollars on health care in Africa and India. The foundation also spent hundreds of millions to develop an AIDS vaccine and a preventive microbicidal gel, as well as more than $17 billion in the United States to develop globally competitive high schools.

In his Harvard commencement address on June 2, 2007, Bill Gates said:

> If you believe that every life has equal value, it's revolting to learn that some lives are seen as worth saving, and others are not. . . . This task is open-ended. It can never be finished. But a conscious effort to answer this challenge will change the world. (Clinton, 2007, p. 14)

Since 1998, Oprah Winfrey's Angel Network has given more than $6 million in Use Your Life Awards to fifty-four small and medium-sized organizations to expand their efforts to help people in need, and the network has provided books for children in nations where an Oprah's Book Club selection exists including China, Columbia, Mexico, Russia, and the United States, particularly in the states of Alabama, Arkansas, and Georgia, and the Gulf Coast areas hit by Katrina. In addition, Winfrey has also established the Oprah Winfrey Leadership Academy for Girls Foundation with $40 million dollars to establish a school for academically gifted but economically disadvantaged girls in South Africa.

The Tiger Woods Foundation planned and developed the Tiger Woods Learning Center in Anaheim on fourteen acres, along with a professional Class A golf course. In addition, the learning center has a 35,000-square-foot education facility. After school and on weekends, students can participate in unique enrichment activities, including forensic science, engineering, robotics, aerospace, video production, and home design. The mission of the Tiger Woods Learning Center is to provide students a broader perspective of the world, an appreciation of their own skills, and opportunities to develop the necessary tools to achieve long-term success. Tiger Woods said kids have big dreams and he is giving them a chance to help realize their dreams.

EMBRACE LIFE WITH A PASSION

These students, adults, and foundations represent people who are living their lives with a purpose and passion. Meyer (2007) in *I Dare You: Embrace Life With a Passion* said there is an innate desire in people to reach for goals, and everyone needs a reason to get up every day and to feel that spark that keeps them motivated and moving.

Inside I'm Standing Up!

We have explored the importance of self-talk and its importance in helping gifted kids to refuse to give up, to develop long-term goals, and to help them move toward identifying and working toward their purpose. Meyer (2007) shared a wonderful story about a little boy who kept standing up in church, and he was warned several times by his mother to sit down. He finally complied, but after a few minutes, he leaned over to his mother and said, "I may be sitting down on the outside, but I'm standing up on the inside" (Meyer, 2007, p. 203).

Gifted kids need to build the courage to continue to stand up on the inside, to reach their goals as adults to lead our nation's transformation, and to help give people a chance to live out their dreams—as well as their own dream to live a meaningful life—and to make a difference.

Focusing Positive Energy to Help Others

Orloff (2004) in *Positive Energy* said giving of yourself to better the lives of others, your community, and the world will help you get out of self and reverse negative energy. Gifted students describe this process as "feeling good." The world is in crisis, with serious social, economical, and environmental repercussions, and gifted kids want to make a difference. To make a difference, gifted kids need to develop a mind-set to carry out their dreams.

MAKE A DIFFERENCE MIND-SET

Tim Drake (2006, p. 42) in *I Want to Make a Difference* provides a comprehensive list of values from various systems. The first step to creating a different mind-set is to scan the list, circle ten values that "ring your chimes," and rank those that you circled from 1 to 10. Once you have identified your top ten values, you can then start to create a *values map*. Drake suggested putting the top ten values on a 3×5 card. You can add drawings and color—be creative and have fun—identifying the top one, followed by the other nine in order. He said to place the top two, three, or four leading values clustered into an arrowhead. This arrowhead gives the overall design a sense of momentum. The list is alphabetical and includes the following values:

Accountability	Dialogue
Ambition	Domain balance (physical,
Behaving morally	emotional, mental, spiritual)
Being competitive	Efficiency
Being creative	Empathy
Being liked	Enthusiasm
Belonging	Fairness
Broad vision	Family
Care for the environment	Flexibility
Caution	Focus
Community service	Forgiveness
Control	Friends
Cooperation	Future generations
Courage	Gentleness

Harmony	Physical exercise
Honesty	Pride
Humor/Fun	Productivity
Image—how others see you	Respect
Independence	Responsibility
Integrity	Reward
Kindness	Security
Knowledge	Self-discipline
Learning	Self-improvement
Love	Social responsibility
Meaning	Status
Nutrition	Trust
Openness	Wealth
Perseverance	Wisdom
Personal development	Work-life balance

After identifying your top ten values, Drake suggested that you put it aside, and write your obituary with your significant achievements and accomplishments. He shared the life story of Alfred Nobel, who had spent most of his life developing weapons in a global business that contributed to the death and maiming of countless numbers of soldiers in the Franco-Prussian War. By mistake, a national newspaper published an obituary of Nobel and he was shocked to see that he was primarily being remembered for his invention of dynamite and the deaths of so many people. He decided to devote the rest of his life to the peace process, and he created the Nobel Peace Prize. Today, Nobel is known globally as an individual who recognizes, rewards, and helps peace happen.

In writing your obituary, focus on the good in your life. This activity will provide you a chance to reassess your priorities and to see if your life so far has been on purpose. One activity that Drake suggested for finding your purpose is to write a letter to a young relative who has asked for your advice concerning what you have found important and uplifting in your life. This is a positive exercise that will encourage you to focus on ways to find fulfillment.

McCain (2007) in *Character Is Destiny* said that an active life serves the purpose of giving an opportunity to realize values in creative work. Examining your values can also direct you to what Beck (2001) calls "finding your North Star." Beck stressed that the knowledge of your perfect or unique lifestyle sits inside you, just as the North Star sits in its own unalterable spot.

Examples of Values Maps

The value map below is that of a 16-year-old gifted student who listed his top ten values as follows:

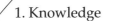

1. Knowledge
2. Behaving morally
3. Being liked

4. Humor/Fun

5. Love

6. Honesty

7. Being creative

8. Forgiveness

9. Personal development

10. Courage

Barry is an academically high achieving gifted student in his high school, and he has a career goal of working in computer graphics. Even though he said, "I pretty much know what I want to do with my life, careerwise, I still want to have fun and be liked." Knowledge is very important to him, and he can always be counted on for an interesting fact or piece of information that he has gleaned from the Internet or NPR. He attended a three-week residential program for gifted kids, and the director said, "Barry served as the in-house computer whiz and downloaded hands-on physics exercises for his physics class, much to the delight of the other students." He has a well-defined sense of who he is, and behaving honestly and morally is important to him. He served as a junior counselor in the summer program, and when student infractions of rules were discussed, he was the first one to talk about forgiveness and giving the students another chance. He drew his arrowhead around the first three values as his momentum point: knowledge, behaving morally, and being liked.

He will need the courage that he listed as number ten to behave morally when his behavior conflicts with group standards, and this may put him in a position in which he may experience not being "liked." Barry's response to the value-map task was, "This was a great and quick way to think about what is important to me. I want to keep on learning, knowledge is important to me, and so is being creative. And I want to be true to myself."

The second value map is that of a 23-year-old graduate student from India who is pursuing a master's degree in civil engineering. Suresh was an instructor in the summer residential program that Barry attended, and he taught a class on Asian appreciation and culture. The students learned about the culture and traditions of a number of Asian countries, including India. Suresh will graduate in December, and he hopes to secure a job in the United States in an engineering firm. His top ten values were as follows:

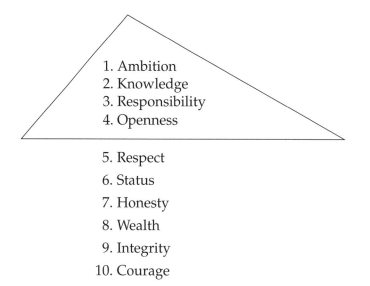

1. Ambition
2. Knowledge
3. Responsibility
4. Openness

5. Respect

6. Status

7. Honesty

8. Wealth

9. Integrity

10. Courage

The top four values that Suresh identified in his values map were ambition, knowledge, responsibility, and openness. These values will make him a valuable employee, someone who wants to learn, be responsible, and be open to new ideas. Ambition will motivate him to keep on learning, and his ambition is reflected in the values of status, respect, and wealth. Integrity will offset the values of status and wealth and help ensure that Suresh is honest in his dealings with his responsibilities at work. He works as a graduate assistant in the College of Education, and his college professor said, "You can always count on him to do a thorough and competent job."

The final values map is that of a college professor in a college of education who is close to retirement. She listed the following values:

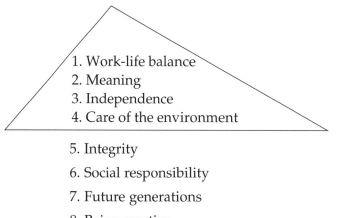

1. Work-life balance
2. Meaning
3. Independence
4. Care of the environment

5. Integrity

6. Social responsibility

7. Future generations

8. Being creative

9. Kindness

10. Learning

The professor said, "I want to establish a work-life balance, and meaning comes to me from my work with teachers in a Quality Teacher Grant Program. These teachers are involved in increasing their content knowledge in science and learning hand-on skills to improve the commitment of their students to become stewards of the environment. She is a highly independent woman and feels a keen sense of social responsibility. She continued, "I believe the transformation of the nation's problems can take place if future generations develop a transformation mind-set." Kindness is essential to her, and this is evidenced in her day-to-day interaction with students, even hand-walking a lost student to their appropriate evening class in another building and engaging that student's professor in light social talk to detract from the lateness of the student.

Difference Making

Activities such as the values map, the obituary, and the letter can help gifted kids and anyone to understand his or her purpose, and to build the skill of difference-making. Drake (2006) said these activities help solve the mystery of who we are and help clarify our values, which represents one of the major ways to understand purpose. An interesting activity for administrators would be to complete a values map for their school, and then values maps for their teachers, to note the congruency of the values of the teachers and the school. In addition, gifted kids could construct a values map and their teacher could construct one, and they could identify where the values of the students and the values of the teacher intersect. Gifted kids want to make a difference, and building a sense of purpose will help ensure that "difference making" becomes a skill they can use to improve relationships, situations, lives, communities, and even societies.

Importance of Being a Role Model

As gifted kids identify their purpose and begin to clarify their values, they can serve as role models for other students. The individuals discussed in this chapter—Eli Winkelman, Freddi Zeiler, President Jimmy Carter, Dr. Wangari Maathai, Muhammad Yunus, Bill and Melinda Gates, Oprah Winfrey, and Tiger Woods—have all developed incredible powerful presences, and they are influencing countless others to make a difference. Having a purpose and understanding that their lives have meaning can bring gifted kids to greater understanding and self-actualization, in which they can become part of something that is so much more important than self.

Drake (2006) calls this process a virtuous circle of improvement, for as people develop a healthy self-concept and feel a sense of self-fulfillment, this in turn makes them healthier, more confident, and more likely to continue to create relevant value for others in the future. The need for gifted kids to add value, improve situations, and make a difference is tremendous, and in the classroom of today there may well be another Chief Joseph, Mohandas Gandhi, César Chavez, Sun Yat Sen, Martin Luther

King, Jr., Eleanor Roosevelt, or countless others who have had a deep yearning to make the world a better place.

SUMMARY

In this chapter, we explored the concept of asynchrony and the importance of parents and teachers understanding the impact of asynchrony on gifted students, as well as the need to help them understand that these differences are normal for them. We examined the research of Le Doux, a pioneering neuroscientist who found that the amygdala can hijack the neocortex and provide the emotions power to disrupt thinking. The need to seek balance in emotional and intellectual intensity was explored, and the role of refocusing to achieve intellectual and emotional balance was discussed. Several ideas to calm the mind, including counting to ten, deep breathing, and visualization, were suggested. Characteristics of gifted kids out of balance and in balance were introduced, as well as the phenomenon of "rushing" as a unique problem of overscheduled gifted kids.

The power of purpose was discussed, as were the ideas of Leider (1997) for creating meaning in your life and work. Finding your purpose was defined as a conscious choice of what, where, and how to make a contribution to the community, to the nation, and to the world. An example of gifted kids finding their calling in Cuba was introduced. Phillip Aaron's idea of exploring aspects of self through self-talk and building efficacy in goal setting were explored, along with a case study of Marta, who used Aaron's book *The Power to Create* as a resource. In discovering your purpose, and more important in living your purpose, you would be moving toward Level V of Dabrowski's Theory of Emotional Development, in which you use your talents to make the world a better place. People with a sense of purpose learn to move their focus away from themselves and focus on others, which represents the higher levels of functioning in the multilevels of Dabrowski (Level IV–V). Level IV includes discovering your purpose and, more important, living your purpose. In Level V you use your talents to make the world a better place.

Finding meaning to life was explored, with examples of students, adults, and foundations that are making a difference. The importance of embracing life with a passion and focusing positive energy to help others was discussed. The work of Tim Drake in *Dare to Be Different* was examined, and his list of values was used to create values maps of a 16-year-old gifted student, a graduate student in engineering, and a college of education professor, as examples of how identifying your values can provide opportunities to focus on ways to find fulfillment. The importance of gifted kids and adults being role models for others was discussed, and the notion of a virtuous circle of improvement was introduced to illustrate how people who develop a healthy self-concept and feel a sense of self-fulfillment, in turn will become more healthy, more confident, and more likely to continue to create relevant value for others in the future.

Teacher Voice

I can see the asynchrony of my gifted students and how important it is to help them achieve balance. I find helping them set reasonable goals is especially helpful—they want to do it all. The example of students finding their purpose was awesome. I will help my gifted students identify areas that they can become passionate about. I also realize that many times we as teachers become frazzled or unglued. We give of ourselves every day to educate and motivate our students. We are not only their teacher, but a parent, nurse, counselor, advocate, and so on. We take them home with us in our hearts every day. Finding balance in our professional, social, and emotional lives is not always easy, but it has to be done. Losing our balance results in losing our purpose, losing our purpose causes us to lose our drive, and once we lose our drive we become just a teacher not an extraordinary facilitator. Find your balance!

Jennifer Babers
Third grade teacher

Read On

Burns, D. (2000). *Feeling good*. New York: Harper Collins.
Goleman, D. (2006). *Social intelligence*. New York: Random House.
Hay, L. (1999). *You can heal your life*. Carlsbad, CA: Hay House.
Jacobs, B. (2004). *Writing for emotional balance*. Oakland, CA: New Harbinger.
Mellin, L. (2004). *The pathway: Follow the road to health and happiness*. New York: HarperCollins.
Neilhart, M. (2006). Can resiliency be taught or is it innate? *Understanding Our Gifted, 19*, 3–6.
Pachter, B. (2000). *The power of positive confrontation*. New York: Marlowe.

Log On

ARK (Absolute Return for Kids) (http://www.arkonline.org/). This Web site provides a brief overview of trends and demographics, and updates access to treatment for transforming the lives of HIV children.

By Kids for Kids (http://www.bkfk.com/). A Web site devoted to helping children develop their innovative spirit and become problem solvers.

Kids to the Rescue (http://www.kidstotherescue.org/). A Web site created by two Minnesota sixth graders focusing on helping children affected by Hurricane Katrina.

Oprah's Angel Network (http://www.oprahsangelnetwork.org/). This Web site describes the purpose and function of the Angel Network.

Oprah Winfrey Leadership Academy Foundation (http://oprahwinfreyleadershipacademy .o-philanthropy.org/). This Web site describes the South African Leadership Academy initiated and funded by Oprah Winfrey.

The U.N. Millennium Development Goals (http://www.un.org/). This Web site lists the United Nation's goals for the next millennium.

Virgin Earth Challenge (http://www.virginearth.com/). This Web site discusses the challenge to individuals to develop and demonstrate viable designs to reduce greenhouse gas.

Reflect On

- Tim Drake said your values map should become a working document that you can refer to daily. Make your own values map. It may take one or two attempts to make it feel right. Leave space for any new values you might want to add that are too far removed from your situation now.

- Think about what you would include in your obituary. What achievements would you want to include? Would a colleague write a different obituary than the one you would write?
- Could the ideas that the Grameen Bank used to make loans be implemented in the United States? If not, why not?
- Joseph Campbell in *The Power of Myth* (Campbell & Moyers, 1988) said when you find your bliss you will meet people on the same invisible track who share your goals. Then he said doors will open for you. Has this happened to you or to someone you know?

REFERENCES

Aaron, P. (1991). *The power to create.* Dallas, TX: Pennington.

Alter, J. (2006). *The defining moment.* New York: Simon & Schuster.

Beck, M. (2001). *Finding your own north star.* New York: Random House.

Burns, D. (2000). *Feeling good.* New York: HarperCollins.

Campbell, J., & Moyers, B. (1988). *The power of myth.* New York: Doubleday.

Clinton, B. (2007). *Giving: How each of us can change the world.* New York: Alfred A. Knoff.

Davidson, R. J. (2004). Well-being and affective style: Neural substrates and biobehavioural correlates. *Philosophical Transactions of the Royal Society (London), 359,* 1395–1411.

Dowla, A., & Barua, D. (2006). *The poor always pay back: The Grameen II story.* Bloomfield, CT: Kumarian Press.

Drake, T. (2006). *I want to make difference.* London: Cyan Books.

Goleman, D. (1996) *Emotional intelligence.* New York: Random House.

Goleman, D. (2006). *Social intelligence.* New York: Random House.

Gore, A. (2006). *An inconvenient truth: The planetary emergency of global warming and what we can do about it.* Emmaus, PA: Rodale Press.

Hay, L. (1999). *You can heal your life.* Carlsbad, CA: Hay House.

Jacobs, B. (2004). *Writing for emotional balance.* Oakland, CA: New Harbinger.

Le Doux, J. (2002). *Synaptic self: How our brains become who we are.* New York: Penguin Putnam.

Leider, R. J. (1997). *The power of purpose: Creating meaning in your life and work.* San Francisco: Berrett Koehler.

Maathai, W. (2006). *Unbowed.* New York: Knopf.

McCain, J. (2007). *Character is destiny.* New York: Random House.

Mellin, L. (2004). *The pathway: Follow the road to health and happiness.* New York: HarperCollins.

Meyer, J. (2007). *I dare you: Embrace life with a passion.* New York: Faithwords.

Neilhart, M. (2006). Can resiliency be taught or is it innate? *Understanding Our Gifted, 18,* 3–6.

Orloff, J. (2004). *Positive energy.* New York: Three Rivers Press.

Pachter, B. (2000). *The power of positive confrontation.* New York: Marlowe.

Schlessinger, L. (2006). *Bad childhood, good life.* New York: HarperCollins.

Shaw, B. (1905). *Man and superman: A comedy and a philosophy.* New York: Cambridge University Press.

Silverman, L. (1998). Through the lens of giftedness. *Roeper Review, 2,* 142–143.

Sisk, D. (1990). *Program report of Cuban visitation.* Spokane, WA: People to People.

Sisk, D., & Shallcross, D. (1989). *Intuition: An inner way of knowing.* Buffalo, NY: Bearly.

Tocqueville, A. (1994). *Democracy in America.* New York: Everyman's Library.

Tolan, S. (1989). Special problems of young highly gifted children. *Understanding Our Gifted, 1*(5), 1, 7–10.

Yunus, M. (1999). *Banker to the poor: Micro-lending and the battle against world poverty.* New York: Public Affairs.

Zeiler, F. (2006). *A kid's guide to giving.* Norwalk, CT: Innovative Kids.

Index

163

CORWIN PRESS

The Corwin Press logo—a raven striding across an open book—represents the union of courage and learning. Corwin Press is committed to improving education for all learners by publishing books and other professional development resources for those serving the field of PreK–12 education. By providing practical, hands-on materials, Corwin Press continues to carry out the promise of its motto: **"Helping Educators Do Their Work Better."**